RENAISSANCE

BY PATRICK HOTLE, Ph.D.

COPYRIGHT © 1998 Mark Twain Media, Inc.

ISBN   10-digit: 1-58037-072-1
        13-digit: 978-1-58037-072-1

PRINTING NO. CD-1302

Mark Twain Media, Inc., Publishers
Distributed by Carson-Dellosa Publishing Company, Inc.

Table of Contents

Introduction

As a student, my first impression of the Renaissance was of an age that suddenly burst upon an unsuspecting Europe. Apparently one day the people of the dreary Middle Ages woke up and realized that they now lived in a happier and more colorful era. The Renaissance certainly seemed more interesting than my own times. Life appeared dull and ordinary in comparison. As I matured, however, I learned about the sophistication of the Middle Ages and realized that the Renaissance was only a continuation of the previous period. I learned that the word *Renaissance* was not even used to describe the fifteenth and sixteenth centuries until 1860. In that year, the Swiss historian, Jacob Burkhardt, began to popularize the idea that those two centuries made up an important and identifiable era in the history of Western civilization. History, in other words, was as much about the names historians used to describe and interpret the past as it was about the past itself. I also learned, with the benefit of hindsight, that the years of my own childhood, the 1960s and 1970s, were anything but dull. Americans like myself grappled with the tensions resulting from the Vietnam War, the civil rights movement, and social revolution. What I perceived, at the time, as confusing and complicated everyday experience later turned out to be the subject matter of history books. No doubt, the people living in the Renaissance felt similarly puzzled by their own times.

My early encounter with history is typical. First, I romanticized the past and did not see myself as part of it. Then, I learned about the tentative nature of historians' interpretations of the past. Finally, I saw myself not as a self-contained individual, but as someone who was primarily formed by historical experience. Only with that knowledge did I begin to grasp a deeper understanding of my own place in history. Therefore, in my small way, I offer this book not only as an aid for exploring the Renaissance, but also as a guide for those who want to move down the path of self-discovery. On such a voyage, only a knowledge of history can enable one to make much progress.

Such a small book can cover only a few topics. However, my selection of topics was based on three objectives. First, I wanted to introduce students to subjects not normally covered in a traditional textbook, like fashion, hygiene, alchemy, education, food, art, music, dancing, and even a little philosophy. Second, I sought to give the reader a basic understanding of the themes seen as important by professional historians. Finally, I wanted to come up with stimulating activities that would persuade students to go more deeply into the study of history. I hope that I have accomplished at least some of these goals.

Although a number of people have assisted me in the writing of this book, two people deserve special thanks. Donna Calvert offered valuable advice on Renaissance dance. Mary Oatman, in addition to constant encouragement and support, spent many hours editing my prose and making it more accessible to middle schoolers. I also benefited from her extensive knowledge of art and art history. Any errors or misjudgments, however, are my own.

—The Author—

Time Line

410	Rome falls to the Visigoths
711	Moslem warriors invade Spain
1099	Crusaders take Jerusalem
1194	Chartres Cathedral completed
1275	Marco Polo serves at the court of Kublai Khan in China
1341	Petrarch is crowned poet laureate in Rome
1348	Black Death strikes Florence
1353	Giovanni Boccaccio completes the *Decameron*
1397	Medici Bank founded in Florence
1402	Gian Galeazzo Visconti, Duke of Milan, dies
1403	Brunelleschi and Donatello go to Rome
1419	Brunelleschi designs dome of Florence Cathedral
1427	Masaccio paints *The Tribute Money*
1430	Donatello casts the statue *David*
1434	Cosimo de' Medici begins 30-year domination of Florence
1455	Gutenberg prints a Bible
1469	Lorenzo de' Medici dominates Florence
1483	Louis XI of France dies
1487	Bartholomeu Dias rounds the southern tip of Africa
1492	Ferdinand and Isabella of Spain capture Granada
1492	Columbus reaches the Americas
1493	Paracelsus born
1494	Lorenzo de' Medici dies
1494	The French invade Italy
1495	Leonardo da Vinci paints the *Last Supper*
1498	Dürer publishes *The Apocalypse*
1498	Vasco Da Gama arrives in India
1504	Michelangelo finishes his *David*
1512	Michelangelo finishes the ceiling of the Sistine Chapel
1513	Machiavelli writes *The Prince*
1516	Erasmus issues his New Testament
1517	Luther posts his 95 theses against indulgences
1521	Hernando Cortes conquers Mexico
1525	Peasant's Revolt in southern Germany is crushed
1527	Castiglione publishes *The Courtier*
1533	Henry VIII weds Anne Boleyn
1535	Death of Isabella d'Este
1536	John Calvin arrives in Geneva
1543	Copernicus publishes his book on the solar system
1547	Edward VI is crowned king of England
1553	Mary I is crowned queen of England
1558	Elizabeth I is crowned queen of England
1563	Council of Trent ends (begun in 1545)
1587	Raleigh founds first English colony in North America
1588	Defeat of the Spanish Armada
1607	Jamestown founded
1608	Galileo constructs telescope to study the heavens
1616	Shakespeare dies
1620	Pilgrims establish Plymouth

Good News for the City of Florence, The Late Middle Ages

Gian Galeazzo Visconti

The messenger choked on the clouds of dust blown in his face. The red and gold colors of Florence that he wore were covered with a coat of dirt and grime. Yet the good news that he bore to his home city made him smile despite the grit in his teeth. The duke of Milan, Gian Galeazzo Visconti, was dead. For 17 years, the duke had used the great wealth of his territories to maintain diplomats, spy networks, and armies in order to conquer the independent Italian city-states. First, all of Lombardy yielded to him, then Genoa, Pisa, Perugia, Siena, and finally, Bologna. Now, only one important independent republic remained: Florence. Unfortunately for Visconti, as he advanced on Florence at the very height of his power, with most of Italy lying at his feet, he suddenly became ill and died. Florence was saved, it seemed, by a miracle. The duke's vision of a united Italy under his control was shattered. With such joyful news, the dust-covered messenger clattered onto the bridge over the Arno River and into the red-roofed city.

Italy at the beginning of the fifteenth century was made up of many tiny, independent **city-states**. City-states were similar to small countries. Some, like Milan, were ruled by ruthless men who seized power by treachery and bloodshed. Others, like Florence, were republics proud of their freedoms. Italy's social and political structure was different from the rest of Europe at the time. Elsewhere, kings were gaining strength and expanding their control over larger territories. Louis XII, known as the spider king because of the webs he wove to trap his enemies, created a powerful French kingdom. The Italians, however, had no king to unite them and resisted men like Visconti who tried. Why was Italy different?

In the Middle Ages (the sixth to fifteenth centuries), most Europeans were part of the **feudal system**. The feudal system was a society based on the common person's need for protection. Wealthy and powerful men known as feudal lords provided that security. The feudal structure took shape after the Roman Empire collapsed in the fifth century. Earlier, Europeans had enjoyed peace and prosperity thanks to Roman military might and administration. However, as the empire weakened and fell, war became a constant problem. In this time of danger, the feudal system evolved to give people protection. Europeans exchanged their land, livestock, and freedoms in return for the right to flee into the local feudal lord's castle when marauders attacked. They were also obliged to serve their noble lord as soldiers.

The Italians responded to the collapse of Roman government differently from other Europeans. Rather than exchange their freedoms and properties for feudal protection, they formed themselves into tiny, self-ruling, independent city-states. Because Italy was more urbanized than the rest of Europe, these states centered around the important city in the region rather than a lord's castle. This meant that feudalism did not take root in Italy.

The Italians were also more active in trade than the rest of Europe. City-states like Venice, Pisa, and Genoa sent fleets of merchant ships to the more sophisticated Islamic and

Byzantine civilizations of the Middle East. There they traded for spices, medicines, and luxurious cloth. At the same time, new ideas in art, technology, science, and philosophy flowed back to Italy through the trade routes.

In addition to having a different social and political structure than the rest of Europe, the Italians were also well-positioned to economically exploit the kingdoms to the north, like France and England. By the late Middle Ages, these kingdoms were gaining power. Warfare had become more costly as powerful monarchs needed bigger armies. The arrival of gunpowder in Europe from China also meant that professional soldiers called **mercenaries** were needed to fire complex new weapons like the cannon and the **arquebus**, an early form of handgun. Kings needed money, and the only place to find it was in Italy. Due to their trade with the Middle East, the Italians had money to lend to their northern neighbors at high interest.

Italian city-states were successful in trade because of their close proximity to the Middle East, but also because they lived in the most well-developed urban environments in Europe. The Roman Empire was an urban empire and believed that civilization needed cities to prosper. Long after Roman government was gone from Italy, the well-planned and fortified cities remained where goods could be safely bought and sold. Along with the city walls and streets, the Romans also left important ideals. Before Rome had become an empire, it had been a republic where parts of the population had a voice in government. Democratic ideals survived the fall of the empire and continued to prosper in the Italian city-states. Citizenship, freedom, and duty were still prized by many Italians in the fifteenth century.

The result of all of these factors at the beginning of the fifteenth century meant that cities like Florence were wealthy, sophisticated, and fiercely independent. They were also deeply religious, another legacy of Rome. The death of the duke of Milan, just as he seemed poised to conquer Florence, was seen as a sign that God approved of the Florentines. It was with tremendous self-confidence, then, that the citizens of Florence embarked on the new century.

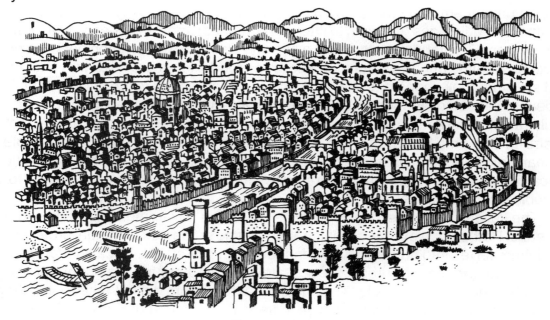

Florence, Italy

Name _____ Date _____

Challenges

1. Who was Gian Galeazzo Visconti? _____

_____

2. How was Italy different from the rest of Europe at this time? _____

_____

_____

3. What did the Roman Empire give Europe? _____

_____

4. Why did feudalism exist? _____

_____

5. What was feudalism? _____

_____

_____

6. Why did kings need more money in the late Middle Ages? _____

_____

7. Why did Italy have more money than the rest of Europe? _____

_____

8. What did Italian traders bring back from the Middle East? _____

_____

9. Why were Italian city-states successful in trade in the late Middle Ages? _____

_____

_____

10. What did the Roman Empire leave behind? _____

_____

_____

Name _____ Date _____

Points to Ponder

1. What advantages did Italy have over the rest of Europe?

_____

_____

_____

_____

_____

2. What weaknesses did Italy have?

_____

_____

_____

_____

_____

3. In addition to wealth, what impact did trade with the Middle East have on Italy?

_____

_____

_____

_____

_____

Name _____ Date _____

Activities

Use a classroom atlas and the blank map of Italy on page 6 to complete the following activities.

A. On the blank map, locate with a dot and label the following cities:
   1. Florence
   2. Siena
   3. Genoa
   4. Pisa
   5. Perugia
   6. Milan
   7. Rome
   8. Ferrara
   9. Naples
   10. Bologna
   11. Venice
   12. Mantua

B. On the blank map, draw in and label these rivers, mountain ranges, and seas:
   1. Arno River
   2. Tiber River
   3. Po River
   4. The Alps
   5. The Apennines
   6. The Adriatic Sea
   7. The Mediterranean Sea
   8. The Tyrrhenian Sea

C. On the blank map, label these islands and countries:
   1. Sicily
   2. Corsica
   3. Sardinia
   4. Elba
   5. The kingdom of France
   6. Switzerland

D. 1. Underline the names of those city-states captured by Visconti.
    2. Circle those city-states that sent fleets of merchant ships to the Middle East.
    3. List on the bottom of your map modern-day countries that share borders with Italy.

Name _____ Date _____

Map of Italy

The Medici Rule, Patronage

Cosimo de'Medici

The only way for the Pazzi family to regain control of Florence was to destroy the Medici family. By April of 1478, they were ready to strike. The signal was to be the ringing of the bell during mass. Just as Lorenzo and Giuliano de' Medici bowed their heads in prayer, the assassin was to strike his dagger into their backs. Yet everything seemed to be going wrong on the appointed day. That morning, the man hired by the Pazzi to do the deed shrank back at the idea of committing murder at the high altar of the cathedral. Two members of the Pazzi family had to take his place. Next, Giuliano de' Medici failed to appear because of a sore knee and had to be roused from his bed and escorted to church. The moment came. As the bell rang out its deep tones, the two assassins leaped upon Giuliano and stabbed him 19 times. Lorenzo, however, escaped into a side room with only a gash on the neck. Within minutes, the city was in arms against the conspiracy. A mob grabbed the Archbishop Salviati, one of the Pazzi's leaders, and hanged him from a window. The murderers themselves were soon strung up beside him. For the next four days, everyone even remotely suspected of sympathizing with the Pazzi was slaughtered or exiled. The Pazzi conspiracy made it plain to all potential rivals of the Medici that the citizens of Florence would not flinch at spilling blood to protect their favorite family.

Who was this Medici family, and why were they so well-loved by the Florentines? Florence was ruled by a council called the **Signory**. It was made up of representatives from the four quarters of the city. However, the priors, as these men were called, held power for only brief periods. They were replaced every two months. Nevertheless, Florentine families like the Pazzi murdered, pillaged, and exiled other families year after year in order to control the Signory. At the beginning of the fifteenth century, one family with great skill and intelligence managed to scramble to the top and stay there despite opposition. They were the Medici.

Medici power relied upon banking. The family had 16 branches in European capitals, which made it one of the richest families in Florence. They were also masterful in earning the support of those less wealthy. The founder of the business, Giovanni spent large amounts of money on churches and hospitals. When he was a member of the Signory, he supported tax reform that helped the poor at the expense of the rich. Because of his generosity, most of the citizens of Florence mourned his passing. His son, Cosimo, was even more successful at politics and business than his father. He established behind-the-scenes control of the Signory. The council made him banker to Florence and special advisor to the government. With these offices, he was in a position to run the city for 30 years. It is important to note that Cosimo could not have stayed in power so long if he had not identified his own interests with the happiness of Florence. He did this well by patronizing the arts.

In addition to financing churches and hospitals like his father, Cosimo also spent money on magnificent palaces, costly furniture, and exquisite works of art, both ancient and modern. He employed the greatest craftsmen, artists, and architects of his day to beautify the city and make it famous throughout Italy. The Medici family also entertained on a grand scale and paid for elaborate celebrations. During the yearly festival of St. John, Florentines were treated to a procession of brightly painted chariots, giants on stilts, people dressed up like pagan gods, Roman generals, and mounted knights dressed in fantastical armor. On one occasion, Florence's greatest architect, Brunelleschi, designed a gigantic float that included a heavenly sphere surrounded by flying angels, which eventually opened up to allow an image of the Angel Gabriel to fly to earth.

Cosimo was only unique in the scale of his patronage. Throughout fifteenth-century Italy, wealthy families and princes used patronage of the arts to earn the allegiance of citizens and the awe of rivals. In fact, generosity was seen as a duty of the wealthy in all countries. It was especially expected from families like the Medici, who had earned their wealth from usury. **Usury** means lending money with interest, and in the fifteenth century, usury was considered a sin by the church. Therefore, banking families in particular felt that they owed a debt to God, which could only be repaid by spending lavishly for the public good. Of course, like Cosimo, they were often encouraged to be generous by the fact that patronage enhanced their power as well.

Cosimo established the Medici so securely that his grandson, Lorenzo, could continue the family's domination of Florence without being challenged. Although being involved in politics was always dangerous in the fifteenth century, as the Pazzi conspiracy showed, Lorenzo enjoyed the power if not the title of a prince. He ruled skillfully and was well-loved. The toothy grins of Pazzi skulls decorating the main gate of Florence were a reminder to all that the power of the Medici family remained unchallenged.

Activities

1. Pretend that the town or city where you live is a modern-day, independent city-state. Imagine yourself to be a rich and powerful person. Also imagine that you have rivals for the domination of the city-state. Using the Medici family as an example, make a list of the ways you would spend your money and the things that you would do to earn the support of the city-state. Explain your choices.
2. Look at the Renaissance palaces and churches pictured in Margaret Aston's *The Panorama of the Renaissance,* J. H. Plumb's *The Horizon Book of the Renaissance,* or John Hale's *The Renaissance.* These books can usually be found in school libraries. Using the pictures in these books as models, design your own palace or church.
3. Pretend you are a newspaper reporter. Write a news article about the Pazzi conspiracy. (Remember, however, that newspapers as we know them did not yet exist.)
4. View Franco Zeffirelli's movie, *Romeo and Juliet.* It does an excellent job of capturing the look and feel of life in a Renaissance city-state.

Name _____ Date _____

Challenges

1. How did the Florentines react to news of the Pazzi conspiracy? _____

_____

2. What was the Signory? _____

_____

3. What were Florentine families like the Pazzi willing to do in order to control the Signory?

_____

4. Why were the Medici one of the richest families in Florence? _____

_____

5. How did Giovanni de' Medici earn the support of those less wealthy? _____

_____

_____

6. How did Cosimo de' Medici run Florence for 30 years? _____

_____

7. Why did the Medici family feel that they owed a debt to God? _____

_____

_____

8. How did the Medici family try to make a good impression? _____

_____

9. Describe two things Florentines may have seen in the procession of the feast of St. John.

_____

_____

10. Cosimo de' Medici left power to his grandson. What was his name? _____

_____

Name _____ Date _____

Points to Ponder

1. Why was the Pazzi family ready to commit murder in order to gain power?

_____

_____

_____

_____

_____

2. How are modern corporations similar to the Medici family?

_____

_____

_____

_____

_____

3. Why do you think Cosimo wanted to control the Signory from behind the scenes?

_____

_____

_____

_____

_____

In the Courtyard of the Medici Palace, The Early Renaissance

Within the courtyard of the Medici palace, only the sound of water could be heard. The splash of the fountain and the cool shadows of the classical colonnade that surrounded the courtyard was a welcome respite from the dust, noise, and heat of the city outside. Lorenzo de' Medici laughed heartily at the wit of one of his guests as he conducted them across the courtyard and into the main gallery. Here, lifelike, ancient statues of Roman emperors and Greek philosophers stood beside a modern sculpture of the biblical story of Judith slaying Holofernes.

Let's join Lorenzo's party and amble through the library. It will tell us a great deal about the Renaissance. You will notice that most of the statues, coins, and cameos were made in ancient Greece and Rome. Historians call that period in history the **classical age**. Lorenzo was deeply interested in classical art and architecture. As we move on through the library, notice also the beautifully bound books of ancient authors and the tapestries of Greek mythology. Lorenzo loved classical literature as much as art and architecture.

People like Lorenzo de' Medici who were passionately interested in the ancient world were called **humanists**. The word itself reveals what it was that the humanists found so attractive in the ancient world. The classical writers believed that humans had great potential for growth in all areas at the same time. They were concerned with living this life to the fullest. A well-lived life should be active in the affairs of the world, yet scholarly and creative. They also believed that the human body, like so much else about humans, was beautiful. This could be seen in the ancient statuary of human figures that found their way into Lorenzo's collection.

So immersed were humanists in the ancient world that they tried to emulate it. As we continue our stroll through the library, notice the marble sculpture of the biblical story of Judith slaying Holofernes. It was done by Donatello, a contemporary of Lorenzo. Obviously, the sculptor looked closely at the surviving statues from the classical world. See how graceful and true to life it is. Observe closely the round painting on the opposite wall by Fra Filippo Lippi, who was another contemporary of Lorenzo. This is called *Adoration of the Magi*. This painter learned how to create life-like images also by studying Roman art work. He built on the Roman artistic traditions to create something new.

Stop and consider the fact that similar things had been happening in literature for a long time. One hundred years before the birth of Lorenzo, the Florentine, Francesco Petrarch (1304–1374) was already living the model of a Renaissance humanist life. He perfected his Latin, collected ancient manuscripts, and even published a book called *Letters to the Ancient Dead*, in which he wrote to the long-deceased classical authors, Homer,

Virgil, and Cicero, lamenting the ignorance of his own day. Petrarch also created some of the most beautiful love poetry ever written. It honored the charms of Laura, a married woman he could only love from afar. In addition to creative endeavors, the Renaissance man was to be active in the affairs of the world. Petrarch was sent on diplomatic missions as far away as the Netherlands.

Another gifted literary figure of early Renaissance Florence was Giovanni Boccaccio (1313–1375). Abandoning his life as a banker, he turned to literature and wrote the *Decameron.* The book is a collection of 100 folk tales, often comic, that describe life in the fourteenth century. Most books of the day were written in Latin. The *Decameron* was unique because it was crafted in Italian. Influenced by his contemporary and teacher, Petrarch, he turned to the classics, collected ancient manuscripts, and wrote essays on famous men and women from the ancient world.

You will note as you walk by the walls of leather-bound books in Lorenzo's library that the creative seeds planted in the fourteenth century by men like Petrarch and Boccaccio established the growth of the Renaissance in fifteenth-century Florence. Leonardo Bruni (1370–1444) translated the two great Greek philosophers, Plato and Aristotle, into Latin. Marsilio Ficino (1433–1499) translated all of Plato's works and founded the Platonic Academy as a place to study philosophy. Without the patronage of Lorenzo's powerful and wealthy family, the Medici, and other families like them, artists and writers would not have been able to continue to cultivate the creativity that thrived in the Renaissance. For example, Bruni began as a tutor in the Medici household, and Ficino was given the use of the Medici summer villa to meet with students.

By the time we emerge out into the sunny courtyard again, we have a good idea of why historians call the age in which Lorenzo lived the Renaissance. *Renaissance* means "rebirth," and as we have seen, it was the classical age that was reborn. However, it is always important to remember that Renaissance artists, writers, and philosophers did not limit themselves to the copying of classical works. Rather, a new vision of life was being born and sculpted by classical thought. So common was this new vision of the world in fifteenth- and sixteenth-century Europe that historians call both of these centuries the Renaissance.

Come, let us move on to the refreshments that our host, Lorenzo, has waiting for us. Let's join in the lively conversation with his guests. Already we can hear an animated discussion of a new translation of one of Plato's works. In time, perhaps we will drift away and sit by the fountain. There, we can pass the late afternoon, pondering the meaning of beauty and listening to the sound of splashing water.

Activities

1. Look at the Apollo Belvedere, the statues of Augustus and Livia, the mummy portrait of a man from Faiyum, the Parthenon, and the Temple of Fortuna Virilis in *Gardner's Art Through the Ages* by R. G. Tansey and F. S. Kleiner (other good art history books will have pictures of these works as well.) Make a list of the main characteristics of classical style revealed in these works and compare your list to the characteristics of today's sculpture and architecture.

2. Find out about the philosophy of Plato by looking at Richard Osborne's illustrated and very accessible *Philosophy for Beginners.*

3. Look at two of Petrarch's love poems printed in J. H. Plumb's *The Horizon Book of the Renaissance.*

Name _____ Date _____

Challenges

1. List three things collected by Lorenzo de' Medici. _____

_____

_____

2. What does the word *Renaissance* mean? _____

_____

3. What was the basis for the Renaissance? _____

_____

_____

4. What is a humanist? _____

_____

_____

5. What did the humanists find so attractive in the ancient world? _____

_____

_____

_____

_____

6. How did Petrarch live the model of a Renaissance life? _____

_____

_____

7. List three classical authors. _____

_____

8. What collection of stories did Giovanni Boccaccio write? _____

_____

9. List two humanists who were patronized by the Medici. _____

_____

Name _____ Date _____

Points to Ponder

1. What impact would a rebirth of the classical age have on today's world?

_____

_____

_____

_____

_____

_____

2. Why do you think the Renaissance began in Italy?

_____

_____

_____

_____

_____

_____

3. Do you agree with the Renaissance humanists that a fully-developed life must be both active in the world and scholarly?

_____

_____

_____

_____

_____

The Bronze Head, The Early Renaissance

Donatello's *David*

The merchant, Nicolo, shook his head. "It's too much. It is truly a beautiful work of art, but you charge too much for your labor." The artist, Donatello, his voice rising, said, "My work in bronze rivals the best artists in Italy and you squabble about price?" Cosimo de' Medici, whom the merchant and artist had called upon to settle the dispute, threw up his hands. Earlier, Cosimo had ordered the life-sized bronze head to be carried to the upper court of the palace and placed overlooking the street, where it could be seen. Nicolo appealed to Cosimo: "It only took him a month to do. At the price he is asking, he would be making over a half florin a day." Donatello turned to the merchant and said, "You are the kind of man who could ruin the fruits of a year's work in a split second." At that, he suddenly shoved the head off the wall. Nicolo and Cosimo gasped as they heard it shatter on the street below.

In the Renaissance, for the first time in history, artists could get away with this kind of behavior. Before, sculptors, painters, and architects were seen as little different from stonecutters or carpenters. That, however, changed in the Renaissance. The wealthy and powerful in Italian city-states competed with each other to hire the finest artists. At a time when the upper classes wanted to create an image of sophistication, the dutifulness and piety of the artist was vital. Only he could paint their portraits as they tried their best to look like devout Christians, ferocious soldiers, or sensitive patrons of the arts.

The artists themselves were shaped by Renaissance ideals. When they talked with humanists or patrons, they learned that the creation of beautiful things was one of the highest goals. As a result, artists like Donatello began to see themselves as more than just craftsmen. They defined themselves as unique individuals because they were creators. Contemporary biographers started using the word "genius" to describe the social spirit of these self-confident men. Most people have accepted the idea ever since. That is why creative individuals are still shown respect today.

Florence had more than its fair share of such creative geniuses. Even in the Middle Ages, the city had been admired for its craftsmanship in gold, silver, and silk. The Florentines already knew a great deal about making beautiful objects. The same workshops that produced exquisite gold jewelry or silver goblets also prepared young artists for a life in painting, sculpture, or architecture. Of course, as soon as a great talent appeared, the Medici family were quick to employ him. The atmosphere in workshops must have been intense as talented young men struggled to master the necessary skills and find new ways of creating beautiful things. At the end of the fourteenth century, a new Renaissance style in art began to emerge in some of these workshops. It was very different from what had been created in the Middle Ages.

The artistic style of the Middle Ages is called **Gothic**. When historians think of the Gothic style, they find it best represented in Gothic cathedrals. Because religion was central to the lives of people, they put tremendous energy and resources into building these structures. The Gothic cathedral was a huge building with soaring towers, high roofs, and pointed arches. Everything about the building was intended to move the viewer's eye upward and away from this earth toward heaven.

The same was true of the sculpture and painting inside. It was more important to tell a biblical story or convey a religious truth than to create an image of the way things looked in real life. The Gothic artist was not interested in portraying humans or landscapes as they looked. He only wanted to use them as symbols to get his point across. As a result, Gothic painting and sculpture, though beautiful, do not try to create a copy in paint or stone of what the eye sees.

In the Renaissance, artists and sculptors were inspired by humanist ideals. Therefore, they wanted to follow in the footsteps of Greek and Roman artists and create images of the world as it ordinarily looked. Yet, they did not just want to do copies of Greek and Roman art. They wanted to revive classical artistic technique so they could portray life as they lived it in the fifteenth century. So, they set about discovering the secrets of classical artists. The place to begin was, of course, with what remained of classical art, and the place to find the most remnants was Rome. In the 1420s, Donatello traveled there with two other friends, Masaccio, the painter, and Brunelleschi, the architect. They studied all that they could find in the ruins of the old city. The people who lived in Rome at the time thought the three friends were crazy, but they studied, measured, and sketched all that they saw. When they returned to Florence, their heads were filled with new ideas. The three friends quickly set to work to practice what they had learned. The artistic world would never be the same.

Activities

1. Look at the chapters on Gothic and classical Art in *Gardner's Art Through the Ages* by R. G. Tansey and F. S. Kleiner. (There are many other excellent art history books that will do as well.) Particularly good examples of Gothic art are the *St. Francis Altarpiece* by Bonaventural Berlighieri, the *Abraham and Three Angels* from the Psalter of St. Louis, and the "Jamb Statues" on Chartres Cathedral. Make a list of the characteristics of Gothic art. Then look at the section on classical art (see the activities on page 12 of this book). Make a second list of the characteristics of classical art. Compare your lists. What are the attractions of each style? Why do you think artists of the early Renaissance were drawn away from the Gothic to the classical?

2. Look at the Gothic sculptures called the "Jamb Statues" on Chartres Cathedral in the book mentioned above. Then look at Roman and Greek sculpture. Finally, look at Donatello's sculptures, *St. George* and *David*. What characteristics of Donatello's sculptures reflect the Gothic influence? What in his sculptures reflects the classical influence?

Name _____ Date _____

Challenges

1. How were sculptors, painters, and architects viewed in the Middle Ages? _____

_____

2. Why were artists important to the wealthy and powerful of Italian city-states? _____

_____

3. Where were young artists prepared for a life in painting? _____

_____

4. What was the artistic style of the late Middle Ages called? _____

_____

5. Where was this style best represented? _____

_____

6. What was Gothic architecture supposed to do to the viewer? _____

_____

_____

7. What was the Gothic artist trying to do? _____

_____

_____

8. What was the Renaissance artist trying to do? _____

_____

_____

9. Where was the best place to go to study classical art and architecture? _____

_____

10. Who accompanied Donatello, and what did they do? _____

_____

_____

_____

Name _____ Date _____

Points to Ponder

1. Compare the personalities of today's popular music stars with artists of the Renaissance, like Donatello.

_____

_____

_____

_____

_____

_____

2. How was Renaissance art different from Gothic art?

_____

_____

_____

_____

_____

_____

3. What does Gothic art tell us about life in the late Middle Ages?

_____

_____

_____

_____

_____

_____

The Dome,
The Early Renaissance

"My dear Francesco, have you heard about the cathedral?"

"Why, no, Paulo."

"This ridiculous fellow, Brunelleschi, wants to build a dome over it!"

"No, you must be in jest. It's too big, and what if it collapses? What humiliation for the Florentines. It is a symbol of the city's independence and pride."

"Truly, Francesco. And what presumption! No one has been able to build a dome that big since the Roman Empire. Nevertheless, the fool has been studying ruins in Rome and proposes to build this thing, and without scaffolding as well!"

"It can't be done!"

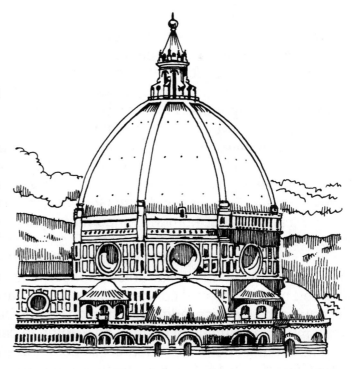

The dome of the Florence Cathedral by Brunelleschi

"Even if Brunelleschi should succeed in putting up some sort of structure, I can assure you that it would fall down in the first wind storm."

Almost six hundred years after conversations very like the above took place, Brunelleschi's dome still dominates the city of Florence. Although at first considered a fool, the Florentines eventually accepted his plan and watched in amazement as the huge, red-tiled dome completed the cathedral in 1436. In the Renaissance, domes were seen as among the greatest achievements of ancient Rome. Nevertheless, before Brunelleschi, they were thought to be impossible to copy. Fifteenth-century Europeans had simply forgotten how to build them. With Brunelleschi's dome, at last the Florentines could consider themselves equal to Rome. The dome rises 180 feet into the air without any visible sign of support. In fact, the dome is really built like a giant umbrella with eight huge ribs that hold it up, but these are hidden within the walls. This was different from medieval cathedrals where structural supports were obvious. For example, the medieval **flying buttress** was a huge arm made of stone that came out from the wall and propped up the cathedral. After the success of the dome, Brunelleschi was asked to design many other churches and public buildings. All reveal the Renaissance desire to create a building that is balanced and harmonious. Renaissance thinkers believed that people needed to be surrounded by beauty in architecture, art, and music.

Just as Brunelleschi used the inspiration of the classical in architecture, his friend, Masaccio, used it in painting. What attracted Masaccio to classical images was their realistic nature. It was Brunelleschi who, by chance, discovered one of the ways classical art achieved this naturalism. While experimenting with geometry and drafting in order to make a model for the dome, Brunelleschi discovered the laws of **linear perspective**. Linear perspective is a method of drawing based on mathematical formulas that enables the artist to create the illusion of a three-dimensional image on a flat surface. The discovery gave Masaccio the ability to make paintings that were more reflective of the natural world. He also used rules of **proportion** when he painted the human form. For instance, when you look at the body of a man from above, his head seems bigger proportionately than his feet, which are farther away. Finally, Masaccio experimented with light and shadow to add to the naturalism and give drama to his subject matter.

His contemporaries were stunned when they saw how he beautifully put all of this together in his fresco, *The Tribute Money*. A **fresco** is a large wall painting on plaster. The subject matter of this fresco is the biblical story of Christ admonishing Peter "to render unto Caesar what is Caesar's and unto God what is God's." The figures in this painting look like anatomically correct human beings moving in a landscape that recedes deep into the background just as it does in real life. Thanks to the added effect of light and shadow, the figures seem like they could have just walked off the street.

Donatello had similar artistic concerns as a sculptor. Like his two friends, he was inspired by the classical concern for naturalism and beauty. He was especially interested in copying the classical admiration for the human body. He was also interested in more than anatomy. In his pursuit of beauty, he wanted to capture the inner life of his subjects, such as their dreams, hopes, and fears. His best-known work is a sculpture of the biblical hero, David, finished in 1430. It was the first free-standing nude sculpture since classical times. David is portrayed as a beautiful adolescent with bony elbows and hand on hip. He is standing triumphantly upon the huge, helmeted head of Goliath, which he has just cut off with a massive sword. Like all Renaissance works of art, the sculpture has many meanings. In addition to the biblical story, the sculpture celebrates the victory of Florence over her enemies. As Renaissance artists and architects created even more beautiful and astonishing works, the Francescos and Paulos of the world were gradually silenced. In the end, they could only stand silently and admire.

Activities

1. Look at the picture of the Florence cathedral in *Gardner's Art Through the Ages* by R. G. Tansey and F. S. Kleiner. Compare it to the picture of the late Gothic cathedral at Cologne on the same page. How does the Florence cathedral differ from the Cologne cathedral?

2. See also the Pazzi chapel designed by Brunelleschi in the book above. Compare it to the classical architecture you observed for the activities on page 12 of this book.

3. Look at Masaccio's painting *The Tribute Money* also in *Gardner's.*... How does it compare with the Gothic painting you looked at for the activities on page 16 of this book? How does Masaccio create the illusion of depth on a flat surface?

Name _____ Date _____

Challenges

1. What year did Brunelleschi finish the dome on the Cathedral of Florence? _____

_____

2. Why had Europeans not built domes for many years? _____

_____

3. How is Brunelleschi's dome like a giant umbrella? _____

_____

4. What was a flying buttress? _____

_____

5. What characteristics did Renaissance architects want their buildings to have? _____

_____

_____

6. Why did they think this was important? _____

_____

7. What is naturalism? _____

_____

8. What did Masaccio use to paint three-dimensional figures on a flat surface? _____

_____

9. What else did Masaccio do to make his paintings look realistic? _____

_____

_____

10. Describe Donatello's best-known work. _____

_____

_____

Name _____ Date _____

Points to Ponder

1. Were Renaissance thinkers right to believe that architecture and music have a major influence on the lives of ordinary people? Consider the present day.

_____

_____

_____

_____

_____

2. Why was it so important for the Florentines to build a dome?

_____

_____

_____

_____

_____

3. Does art have to be naturalistic to be beautiful?

_____

_____

_____

_____

_____

Leonardo da Vinci, The Renaissance Man

Leonardo da Vinci

"Master, come look at this."

Verrocchio, master painter, sculptor, and goldsmith, moved across the room to his current painting. When he saw the picture, he gasped. Like most master painters, Verrocchio took on young apprentices to help him with his work and to educate the next generation of artists. He would often do the main sections of the painting and leave details of landscape or minor figures to his apprentices. He had just completed a baptism of Christ and left the angels surrounding the main subject to young Leonardo da Vinci. Verrocchio was stunned when he saw Leonardo's angel. It was more alive than anything he had ever painted. Verrocchio thought to himself, "I won't be deeply saddened when this pupil leaves."

Fourteen-year-old Leonardo da Vinci arrived in Florence in 1466, at the height of the Renaissance. Although he had grown up in the small town of Vinci, his father sent him to the nearby city for education. For eight years, Leonardo studied under Verrocchio and astonished his master with his ability to look closely at life and capture it on canvas. At the age of 20, Leonardo left Verrocchio's workshop and began to work on his own. He produced some of the world's best-known paintings. For instance, his *Mona Lisa,* though much faded from its original bright colors, still seems alive and continues to mystify viewers with her enigmatic smile.

Leonardo, however, was more than a great painter—he sought the secrets of life. We know a great deal about what went on in Leonardo's mind, thanks to his notebooks. Almost 5,000 pages survive. In them, we learn that he wanted to know how things moved. He drew detailed studies of birds in flight, carefully drawing the bones, muscles, and tendons of the wing. He was also interested in engineering and mechanics. Plans for irrigation schemes, central heating, machine guns, submarines, tanks, and life preservers survive. His interest in flight led him to design airplanes and parachutes. Although Leonardo's helicopter would not have flown, many of his other discoveries would have worked if they had been built. His desire to know also led him deep into the study of botany, geology, and astronomy.

Leonardo's determination to look closely at the physical world and learn only from what he could see was a new way of gaining knowledge. At the time, when thinking people looked at nature and tried to understand it, they relied on ancient authorities. For example, medical doctors relied on the theories of Aristotle, who lived 1,800 years before the Renaissance. With Aristotle's works to support them, doctors believed that the human body's health was maintained by the balance of the four humors. These were hot, cold, wet, and dry. Sickness occurred when one of these humors dominated the rest. The prospect of actually cutting open a cadaver to see how the body worked as medical students do today would have been greeted with horror by a fifteenth-century physician. Leonardo had no such

           23

qualms, however, and dissected at least 30 cadavers in order to understand human anatomy.

He also tried to understand the nature of paint. Disastrously, Leonardo experimented with new ways to mix and apply pigments. At first, his results were startling. Artists from all over Italy came to admire the colors in his masterpiece, the *Last Supper*. Almost at once, however, it began to flake away. Many of his paintings have completely disappeared, and the *Last Supper* as seen today is a shadow of its former breathtaking beauty. Innovation and experimentation always require risks, and Leonardo was never one to balk at the unknown.

At other times, it wasn't the danger of the experimentation but bad luck that haunted Leonardo. His clay form for a gigantic bronze statue of the Duke of Milan, Francesco Sforza, was used as target practice by invading French soldiers before it could be cast in bronze. His other employers were often uninterested in his ideas. Sadly, the works Leonardo left behind are few. About a dozen finished paintings, parts of statues, and his notebooks are all that remain. He spent the last four years of his life as guest of the King of France. From his notebooks, we can see that he thought of himself as a failure. "Tell me if anything at all was done…" was written on page after page.

If success is judged by quantity of works completed, then perhaps Leonardo was a failure. If success is judged by innovation, however, then he can rank at the top. He left to the world three discoveries. First, we can command nature when we understand her. Second, we must learn about nature by observation. Third, the physical world cannot be understood by relying solely on all-encompassing theories, but rather by close observation of detail. It is the details that ultimately test the truth of a theory.

In an age that believed that human beings had endless potential for growth, Leonardo came closest to realizing that ideal. His curiosity was boundless.

Activities

1. Look at Leonardo da Vinci's works in *Gardner's Art Through the Ages* by R. G. Tansey and F. S. Kleiner (any good art history book will do). Also look at selections from da Vinci's notebook in *The Horizon Book of the Renaissance* by J. H. Plumb. How does da Vinci differ from Masaccio whose work you looked at for the activities on page 20 of this book? Why do you think that the *Mona Lisa* is so well-known?

2. Notice the lines that da Vinci used to create an illusion of depth on a flat surface in his *Last Supper*. Where do the lines converge? Why did he pick this point?

3. Look at the section on Aristotle's ideas in *Philosophy for Beginners* by R. Osborne.

Name _____ Date _____

Challenges

1. Who was Leonardo's teacher? _____

_____

2. How did Leonardo's teacher know that he had a talented pupil? _____

_____

3. What are the names of some of the best-known paintings in Western civilization painted

by Leonardo? _____

_____

4. What surviving written source tells us about the way Leonardo thought? _____

_____

5. List five of Leonardo's inventions. _____

_____

6. What was new about the way Leonardo gained knowledge? _____

_____

7. What did medieval doctors believe caused illness? _____

_____

_____

8. Which of Leonardo's experiments ended disastrously? _____

_____

9. Where did Leonardo spend his last years? _____

_____

10. What three discoveries did Leonardo leave to the world? _____

_____

_____

_____

_____

Name _____ Date _____

Points to Ponder

1. Why is it necessary to observe nature closely in order to understand it?

_____

_____

_____

_____

_____

2. Do you think that Leonardo's careful observation of the world helped him to paint? Explain.

_____

_____

_____

_____

_____

_____

3. How was Leonardo an ideal Renaissance man?

_____

_____

_____

_____

_____

Michelangelo and the High Renaissance

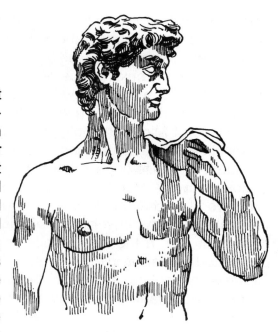

Michelangelo's *David*

It was a bright, warm, October afternoon, yet the citizens of Florence were depressed and worried. They peered out of shuttered windows upon empty streets. All was silent as the city waited for the arrival of the French. Pietro de' Medici, the latest in that family to dominate Florence, had not inspired confidence like his father, Lorenzo. He also had bad luck. In 1494, the French king, Charles VIII, crossed the Alps with 30,000 armored knights, pikemen, archers, and a large train of artillery. When this huge force approached the boundaries of Florentine territory, Pietro de' Medici did not try to resist. He quickly surrendered the castles surrounding the city. On word of Pietro's betrayal, the Florentines rose up, drove the Medici from the city, and pillaged the priceless treasures in the Medici palace. Nevertheless, it was too late to do anything about the French. As the late afternoon sun lengthened the shadows on the narrow streets, the Florentines began to hear the clatter of thousands of horses' hooves on pavement.

The French invasion had a profound impact on the Renaissance in Italy. Florence ceased to dominate the artistic world as the artists fled to the rival cities of Venice and Rome. Meanwhile, the rest of Italy became a battle ground for the great European powers. Once the French began to lay claim to Italian territory, their rivals, the Spaniards, were forced to intervene against them. The dozens of separate Italian states desperately clung to their independence by siding with one group or the other.

Despite almost 40 years of war in Italy, artistically and culturally the early sixteenth century was not all bad. Europeans involved in the wars carried Renaissance ideas, styles, and techniques back with them to their home countries. Some of the world's greatest geniuses continued to produce masterpieces in this tense environment. One of the greatest was Michelangelo Buonarroti.

Michelangelo was born in 1475 and, like so many other talents of the Renaissance, began his training as an artist in the Medici household. After the fall of the Medici in 1494, he left Florence for Rome. Michelangelo shared Leonardo da Vinci's passion for human anatomy, but otherwise the two were very different. Where Leonardo was interested in many things and finished little, Michelangelo was interested in one thing, art, and left a huge amount of completed work. His capacity for production was staggering, and he did not stop until his death at the age of 89.

Michelangelo's particular passion was sculpture. He was also a deeply religious man and wanted to capture in stone the struggle of the human spirit as it grows toward God. He believed that life was like a block of uncarved marble, and the soul was trapped within it. Every human being, like a tireless artist, had to work at releasing the soul's potential perfection from the rock. The human body revealed all that there was to say about beauty and the growth of the soul. The best example of Michelangelo's fascination with human perfection is his sculpture of the biblical hero, David. This image of a more-than-perfect male nude towers 18 feet above the floor. Michelangelo exaggerated many of David's features, like his hands and bulging muscles, in order to convey the impression of power, energy, and skill. To the Florentines, David was a symbol of their independence and courage, but to Michelangelo, he also represented the potential beauty and grandeur of the human spirit.

One of Michelangelo's greatest works is the painting of the ceiling of the Sistine Chapel in Rome. The painting covers approximately 6,300 square feet and contains over 300 larger-than-life figures. He took on the job under protest, complaining that he was a sculptor, not a painter. Yet, this glorious chapel ceiling is one of the most admired paintings in the world. Michelangelo was offered assistants, but he refused them, preferring to paint the vast subject by himself. Most of it he painted while on his back in the midst of scaffolding, dozens of feet in the air. Despite sickness, exhaustion, and supreme discomfort, he completed the ceiling in four years. Michelangelo tells the story of the first book of the Bible, Genesis, in eight huge panels. The painting, however, is to be read opposite to the book. Michelangelo wanted the viewer to begin with the drunkenness of Noah and end with Creation. Just as in his sculptures, Michelangelo was trying to convey the journey of the human spirit back to God. Along the sides, colossal figures of prophets and prophetesses foretell the coming of Christ. Each figure is a masterpiece, and people are often struck by how sculptural the figures are, even though they have been created in paint.

By the time Michelangelo finished the Sistine Chapel in 1512, the long years of warfare had dramatically altered the mood of Italy. The optimism about human potential for growth had given way to pessimism about the future. Michelangelo continued to create breathtaking works of art for another 52 years, but his images of human perfection seemed more and more remote from life as it was led in the sixteenth century.

Activities

1. Look at Michelangelo's *David* in *Gardner's Art Through the Ages* by R. G. Tansey and F. S. Kleiner (other good art history books will do). Compare it to Donatello's *David*, which you looked at in the activities on page 16 of this book.

2. Look at the ceiling of the Sistine Chapel in the above book. Write a brief description of what is occurring in each of the central panels. Also look at the before and after pictures of the recent restoration of the chapel on the following page.

3. Pretend you are a tourist in Rome at the time when Michelangelo is finishing the chapel. Write a letter home describing your response to the ceiling.

4. View *The Agony and the Ecstasy* starring Charlton Heston. The movie is about the painting of the Sistine Chapel and gives students a good feel for the Renaissance in Rome.

Name _____ Date _____

Challenges

1. Why was Pietro de' Medici considered a traitor? _____

_____

2. How did the Florentines respond to Pietro's treachery? _____

_____

_____

3. What two great European powers fought for control of Italy? _____

_____

4. How did the Italian city-states try to survive these invasions? _____

_____

5. How was Michelangelo similar to other Italian Renaissance artists? _____

_____

6. What was Michelangelo's particular passion? _____

_____

7. How did Michelangelo describe his life? _____

_____

_____

_____

8. What work of art is the best example of Michelangelo's fascination with human perfection? _____

_____

9. How large is Michelangelo's painting on the Sistine Chapel ceiling? _____

_____

10. What is the subject of Michelangelo's painting on the Sistine Chapel ceiling? _____

_____

_____

Name _____ Date _____

Points to Ponder

1. What does Michelangelo mean when he describes life like a block of marble with the soul trapped inside?

_____

_____

_____

_____

_____

2. Why did Renaissance artists paint and sculpt mainly religious subjects?

_____

_____

_____

_____

_____

3. If you were going to create an image of human perfection today, who would you use and how would you portray him or her?

_____

_____

_____

_____

_____

Education and the Renaissance Woman

A group of brilliantly-dressed riders slowly emerged from the woods. Among them were ladies-in-waiting, pages, secretaries, and a few soldiers. They were the duchess of Milan's escort for her daily ride. Yet, the young duchess was nowhere in sight. She and her closest companions had held their horses back, supposedly to watch a pair of young foxes scampering in the brush. Their barely hidden smirks revealed other intentions. Suddenly, with whoops of laughter, they furiously galloped down upon the slow-moving escort. The unsuspecting ladies-in-waiting were taken completely by surprise. Two ladies were thrown from their horses and found themselves sitting painfully in the middle of the road,

Isabella d'Este

their brocade dresses, lace, and pearls now covered in dust. Amid moans and curses, the duchess and her friends howled with laughter.

The story above is typical of Beatrice d'Este, one of the most interesting women of the Renaissance. In addition to a rather cruel sense of humor, typical of the fifteenth century, she was also a highly intelligent and talented woman. Unfortunately, she died in giving birth at the age of 22, also typical of the fifteenth century. Her sister, Isabella, however, lived well into her sixties and was described by admirers as the first lady of the world. She and her sister came from the city-state of Ferrara, where her father, Ercole d'Este, was duke. Ferrara of the d'Estes, like Florence of the Medicis and much of the rest of Italy, was caught up in the cultural world of the Renaissance. The duke and duchess of Ferrara were well-known for their patronage of artists and writers. Ferrara was particularly famous for its humanist schools, where those lucky enough to attend received the best education possible.

Humanists had as great an impact upon education as they had on art. Modern education began in the Renaissance. Humanists believed education should be well-rounded and include education of the mind and the body. Therefore, students studied history, literature, grammar, rhetoric, logic, music, arithmetic, geometry, and natural science, but they also studied swimming, dancing, riding, and fencing. Of course, the most important of these was the study of Greek and Latin literature. Students memorized the works of classical authors like Cicero and Quentillion. They then worked on perfecting their own Latin. Humanists believed that the amount a student learned depended upon age and ability, so teachers needed to adapt what and how they taught. In addition, students were also to develop good manners, sound character, and the art of clever conversation.

This humanist education, however, was designed primarily for the upper classes, who made up a small percentage of the population. The majority of the population in the Renaissance was illiterate. The complete education was also intended mainly for boys. Even most upper-class girls had access to only part of it. They learned a smattering of classical literature, music, and dance, but they spent most of their time learning how to manage a house, do needlework, be religious, and be charming, decorous, and submissive wives. Universities were completely closed to women.

Nevertheless, a few determined women did manage to overcome their disadvantages and become writers like Christine De Pizan. She published a book called *The Book of the City of Ladies*, in which she argued that women could do all the jobs necessary to the running of a city. Other women, like Vittoria Colonna, became well-known poets. Still other women, like Artemisia Gentileschi, became successful artists. Such women, however, were rare, and Isabella and Beatrice were two of the very few women even from the ruling classes to enjoy the advantage of a full Renaissance education.

Women received little education because their role in fifteenth-century society required little. To the ruling families of Renaissance Italy, like the d'Este and the Medici, daughters were important for only two reasons. First, they were married to neighboring princes by their fathers in order to create political alliances. Second, they were supposed to give birth to children to keep the family alive. The same was true in the families of ordinary merchants or shop keepers. Women, themselves, had very little choice in the matter. Beatrice, who was mentioned earlier, was married to the 40-year-old duke of Milan when she was 15. Her sister, Isabella, was married at 16 to another prince, the marquis of Mantua, who was older than she, but somewhat closer to her own age. The d'Este women's experience was common. Most women in the Renaissance were married between the ages of 13 and 16 to older men. Although Isabella had no say in the selection of her husband, she went on to live a full and influential life. To Mantua, Isabella attracted the best artists and writers. She also worked at gathering one of the finest libraries in Italy. To cultivate her mind, she wrote and received letters from family, friends, artists, merchants, and thinkers from all over Europe. Over 2,000 of her letters survive.

In 1494, just four years after her marriage to the Marquis, Italy was invaded by a huge French Army under the king of France. As a result, for the rest of Isabella's life, Italy was a battle ground where France, Spain, and Germany fought for domination. The little Italian city-states like Mantua struggled to maintain their independence as best they could between the competing armies. During this time, Isabella's husband was captured, and she was left to rule Mantua alone. She turned out to be far better than her husband at the dangerous game of politics. She ruled so well that her husband even became jealous of her success. Through skillful diplomacy and strict control of the army, she kept Mantua free from attack and peaceful. When her husband died, she continued to rule for her son and eventually even won for him the title of Duke.

As impressive as Isabella was, it is important to remember that she had more opportunities than most women of her day. The vast majority of talented women had to make do with much less. Even her sister, Beatrice, like so many, enjoyed only the limited possibilities of a sadly brief life.

Name _____ Date _____

Challenges

1. From where did the d'Este sisters come? _____

_____

2. How did Beatrice die? _____

_____

3. What did humanists believe about education? _____

_____

4. What subjects did students study in the Renaissance? _____

_____

_____

5. What were the most important subjects? _____

_____

6. Who had the benefit of a humanist education? _____

_____

7. What was education like for most girls? _____

_____

_____

_____

8. Why were daughters important to the ruling families of Renaissance Italy? _____

_____

_____

9. When and to whom were most women of the Renaissance married? _____

_____

10. How did Isabella keep Mantua free from attack during her husband's captivity? _____

_____

_____

Name _____ Date _____

Points to Ponder

1. Compare your education today with an education in the Renaissance. How much has changed?

_____

_____

_____

_____

_____

2. Why do you think a woman's education was so limited in the Renaissance?

_____

_____

_____

_____

_____

3. Why was the sense of humor in the fifteenth century so often cruel?

_____

_____

_____

_____

_____

Name _____ Date _____

Activities

1. Find out more about the lives and works of Christine De Pizan, Vittoria Colonna, and Artemisia Gentileschi. (A good place to look is in J. W. Zophy's *A Short History of Renaissance and Reformation Europe*.)

2. Watch the movie, *The Prince of Foxes,* based on the book by Samuel Shelleburger. It tells the story of an ambitious politician who strives for power in the world of Renaissance city-states.

3. Use the sixteenth-century alphabets below to write your name and a short message.

Capitals

("I" and "J" are the same)

("U" and "V" are the same)

Lower-case Letters

a or ∫ (used at the beginning or in the middle of a word) ß (used only at the end of a word)

The Life of the Lower Classes in the Renaissance

He lowered his head to enter the peasant hut. It was dark and smelly inside. There were no windows and no chimney, so the smoke of the cooking fire mingled with the smell of unwashed humans and the two cows who lived in a small barn just off of the hut. Only a fence kept the animals out of the family's living space. The floor was dirt. As he sat down on the rough hewn bench, he could hear the rustling of rats moving above in the thatched roof. On the table, his wife, who had come in from the fields only a little earlier than he to make supper, placed coarse, black rye bread, dried beans, and a hunk of cheese. A little golden light crept into the open door as the sun set on another ordinary day for the peasant.

For the vast majority of Europeans in the fifteenth century, the picture above was typical. Only a small minority were in a position to enjoy the new ideas, arts, and architecture of the Renaissance. The rest of Europe lived the same way it had for hundreds of years. Most dwelt in the countryside in small villages of 500 to 700 people. Society there was divided into rigid social classes with very little opportunity to move out of them. Two percent of the population belonged to the nobility. Another two to four percent were priests, monks, or nuns. The rest of the population were peasants.

A peasant's life was hard. Every able-bodied person in a peasant family, including women and children, spent most of their days working in their landlord's fields. They aged rapidly and were often bent over from years of hard labor. They had bad teeth and were frequently ill from malnutrition. Seldom did they bathe. Typically, mothers sewed their daughters into their dresses for the winter. Fruit was too expensive, and green vegetables and meat were rare. When crops failed, they might eat seeds, acorns, tree bark, or grass. Starvation was common. During years of bad harvests, more babies than usual were abandoned on roadsides. Even in good years, an estimated one-third of all babies born died in their first year. Under half of those who survived made it to adulthood.

Before the fifteenth century, when a feudal lord of the Middle Ages acquired new property, he could count on a certain number of peasants bound to the land. By the fifteenth century, feudalism was disappearing in western Europe. Little, however, had changed. Although now free to leave the land, most peasants chose to remain rather than face danger and starvation on the road. That meant that they still paid a large part of their harvest to landlords in rent. In addition, they owed a tithe, which was a tenth of their harvest, to the church, and probably more to tax collectors.

This life of drudgery was broken up by church holidays, weddings, seasonal rituals, and occasional fairs. In the fifteenth century, fairs were places where traveling peddlers and merchants could sell their goods. Fairs allowed a peasant family to buy a few small items, socialize with neighbors, drink, and dance. Observers were often shocked by the wildness of peasant dances. However, this exuberance is not surprising, considering that it was one of the peasants' few outlets. Sometimes frustration was released in other ways. Major peasant revolts broke out repeatedly in the fourteenth, fifteenth, and sixteenth centuries. These rebellions were always brutally crushed by the authorities.

Life was somewhat better for ordinary people in cities. During the Renaissance, as we have seen in previous chapters, town dwellers were more likely to be exposed to beautiful architecture, art, and ideas. The cities of the Renaissance were small by today's standards. The biggest were rarely more than 100,000 people. Here, five to six percent of the population were wealthy merchants who dominated the city, much like the Medici did in Florence. Below them, small merchants, shopkeepers, artisans, lawyers, and teachers made up another 50 to 60 percent. At the bottom of this social structure was a third of the town's population. This portion was made up of young apprentices studying trades, gardeners, servants, unskilled laborers, peddlers, and beggars.

All cities in the Renaissance were enclosed by walls, so life was cramped. Most people lived in small, half-timbered apartments above their shops. Only a few, like the wealthy Medici, could build luxurious stone or brick town houses. Streets were often unpaved, narrow, and crooked. A pedestrian would have to find his way around open sewers, goats, cows, pigs, peddlers, and wagons. He or she would also have to be wary about the garbage and human excrement thrown out of windows. At night, without the benefit of street lights, cities were dark and dangerous. Most mornings would see a body or two fished out of the river. To fight crime, punishment was severe, and entrances to towns were often decorated with the heads of executed criminals.

Not surprisingly, city life could be as unhealthy as life in the country. This was especially true of disease. The close quarters and unhealthy atmosphere of cities account for the effects of the Bubonic Plague, better known as the Black Death. This disease was carried by fleas on rats. Cities in the late Middle Ages and Renaissance had huge populations of these rodents living off garbage and nesting in rafters. Infected fleas easily dropped onto the humans below. This killed approximately one-third of Europe's population between 1348 and 1350. Subsequent outbreaks continued to limit Europe's population. One hundred and fifty years later, the population of most cities was still only 60 to 75 percent of what it had been before the plague.

It is important to remember, then, that the breathtaking buildings, exciting ideas, and inspiring paintings were enjoyed by only a few. For the rest, life in the Renaissance was just a daily struggle to keep desperation at bay and stay alive.

Activities

1. Write a skit describing a day in the life of an ordinary peasant.

2. Look at paintings of sixteenth-century peasant life by Peter Bruegel in *Gardner's Art Through the Ages* by R. G. Tansey and F. S. Kleiner (other art history books will do). What do the pictures tell you about the life of a peasant?

3. Pretend you are a concerned citizen of a sixteenth-century city. Write a letter to the town council describing the problems of city life and recommending changes.

Name _____ Date _____

Challenges

1. Where did most people live in the Renaissance? _____

_____

2. Why were peasant lives so hard? _____

_____

_____

3. Even with the end of feudalism, why did little change for the peasant? _____

_____

_____

4. What broke up the life of drudgery for the peasant? _____

_____

5. Why was life somewhat better in the cities? _____

_____

6. How big were the biggest cities in the Renaissance? _____

_____

7. Why was life so cramped in cities? _____

_____

8. Describe a typical street in a city during the Renaissance. _____

_____

_____

9. Why were cities so dangerous? _____

_____

10. What did the Black Death do to Europe? _____

_____

_____

Name _____ Date _____

Points to Ponder

1. Why were peasant dances so wild?

_____

_____

_____

_____

_____

_____

2. What other problems, in addition to plagues, did Renaissance cities have?

_____

_____

_____

_____

_____

_____

3. What created social classes in the Renaissance?

_____

_____

_____

_____

_____

_____

The Northern Renaissance

Albrecht Dürer

When Albrecht Dürer came upon the whale, the creature was nearly dead. For four days, it had been trapped in the saltwater marshes of Zeeland, and people had rushed to see it. Now, exhausted from its struggle and starving, the whale waited quietly for the end to come. Even in death, the huge bulk of the whale was terrifying. The slightest movement of the poor animal sent sightseers scurrying up the dunes in panic. Chuckling to himself at the curses and screams resulting from the whale's latest splashing, Dürer took his pad and water colors from the saddle bag. He studied the whale from every angle, allowing his eyes to absorb every tiny, astonishing detail of the great beast. What amazing wonders nature offered for those who would take the time to look, he thought to himself as he sat down and began to paint.

Like his Italian counterparts Donatello and Brunelleschi, Albrecht Dürer began life as an apprentice to a goldsmith. However, Dürer was German, and, in the north, the historical phenomenon known as the Renaissance was evolving in very different ways. When Dürer became an apprentice in 1486, new forms of painting had appeared in northern Europe, but they were largely unaffected by southern influences. Characteristics of Gothic art, a style that began in the Middle Ages, still dominated the workshops of German cities like Nuremburg, where Dürer studied. Gothic art, no less beautiful than later styles, tended to look mystical and dream-like. Spatial proportions often appeared unnatural in order to emphasize the symbolic importance of a figure. It was this artistic tradition that initially shaped and formed northern Renaissance art, rather than the classical ideals that were thriving in the south.

In time, however, artists like Dürer were compelled to travel to Italy in order to study firsthand the new ideas and techniques that were growing out of the classical past. Dürer journeyed south to Venice, where he became friends with Giovanni Bellini, the leading painter of the city. Bellini showed Dürer techniques for drawing realistically, which would have included such ideas as spatial harmony, linear perspective, and anatomical proportion. Others in Venice exposed Dürer to the Renaissance admiration for Greek and Roman literature. Dürer returned to Nuremburg six months later, full of new ideas that profoundly affected the development of his drawing and print-making.

The Renaissance spread through Germany, France, the Netherlands, and England as men like Dürer returned from their travels with new ideas and techniques. Germany, for instance, was fertile ground for the cultivation of humanist ideals because it had characteristics common to Italy. Like Italy, Germany was divided into dozens of independent states. Also like Italy, these German states thrived on trade and rich banking families like the Fuggers of Augsburg, who were willing patrons of the arts. In addition, the Germans had long been fascinated by the natural world. The forest and meadow played a significant role

40

in its legends, myth, and art. As a result of these pre-existing conditions, Italian ideas easily took root and flourished. However, it is important to remember that, in spite of these similarities, the Renaissance in northern Europe maintained a slightly different texture than in Italy.

Consider the difference in religious practice. In the fifteenth century, there was only one church, which was controlled by the Pope in Rome. Christianity had not yet split into Protestant and Catholic churches. However, northern Europeans, like the Dutch and Germans, were more devout than the Italians. In their view, the Bible was by far the most important book in existence, because it was the primary guide for living a religious life.

The New Testament of the Bible was originally written in Greek. Centuries later, it was translated into Latin, which was the language of the scholars. This translation became known as the **Latin Vulgate**. Since few people could read and understand Latin, people relied on priests to interpret the Vulgate Bible for them. As knowledge of Greek and Latin began to spread north due to the Renaissance passion for understanding classical writing, German and Dutch scholars began to criticize the way the Bible had been translated and inter-

Desiderius Erasmus

preted by the church. People like Desiderius Erasmus, a Dutch humanist, even published a New Testament in Greek, which sometimes differed in meaning from the Latin Vulgate. This caused humanists living in northern Europe to disagree with the church over the nature of religious life and how it should be practiced.

Unwittingly, Erasmus and others like him planted the seeds for a cataclysmic event called the Reformation. Before it was over, Europe would be split into opposing sides and its soil soaked with blood.

Name _____ Date _____

Challenges

1. What artists were counterparts of Albrecht Dürer? _____

_____

2. Name and describe the tradition that influenced northern art before the Italian Renaissance. _____

_____

_____

3. What did Germany and Italy have in common? _____

_____

_____

_____

4. Where did Dürer go in Italy? _____

_____

5. What did Dürer learn in Italy? _____

_____

6. Describe Christianity in the fifteenth century. _____

_____

7. What was the Vulgate? _____

_____

8. What impact did the knowledge of Greek and Latin have on German and Dutch scholars?

_____

_____

9. Who was Desiderius Erasmus? _____

_____

10. What caused the humanists to disagree with the church over what a religious life should be? _____

_____

Name _____ Date _____

Points to Ponder

1. Why did the Germans react differently from the Italians to Renaissance ideas?

_____

_____

_____

_____

_____

2. How was Gothic art different from Italian Renaissance art? How was it similar?

_____

_____

_____

_____

_____

3. Why was religion so important in the late Middle Ages (the fifteenth century)?

_____

_____

_____

_____

_____

Name _____ Date _____

Activities

1. Good examples of the kind of art that northern Europeans were producing in the early fifteenth century are Robert Campin's *The Merode Altarpiece* and Jan van Eyck's *The Virgin with the Canon van der Paele*. They can be found in *Gardner's Art Through the Ages* by R. G. Tansey and F. S. Kleiner. What do these two works tell you about the way fifteenth-century northern Europeans lived and what they valued?

2. Use the blank map of Europe provided on page 45 for the following activities.

   A. On the map provided, locate with a dot and label the following cities:
      1. Florence
      2. Venice
      3. Milan
      4. Augsburg
      5. Nuremburg
      6. Cologne
      7. Prague
      8. Vienna
      9. Amsterdam
      10. Brussels
      11. Wittenburg
      12. Berlin

   B. On the map provided, draw in and label these rivers, mountain ranges, and seas:
      1. North Sea
      2. Mediterranean Sea
      3. Baltic Sea
      4. Adriatic Sea
      5. Rhine River
      6. Danube River
      7. Elbe River
      8. The Alps

   C. On the map provided, label these areas or countries:
      1. Saxony (part of modern-day Germany)
      2. Zeeland (part of the Netherlands)
      3. The Netherlands
      4. France
      5. Denmark
      6. Poland

Name _____ Date _____

Map of Renaissance Europe

The Printing Press

Four grim horsemen gallop over the bodies of dying men and women. First comes Death, riding a bony horse with wild eyes. Then comes Famine, swinging scales like a battle ax. Next comes War, with massive sword held high and ready to strike. Finally comes Plague, who draws a bow and strikes down the human race. This is the frightening version of the Four Horsemen of the Apocalypse as described in the book of Revelation. This is also the image that the German artist, Albrecht Dürer, printed onto a piece of paper.

A printing press in the Netherlands, 1628

Dürer's book, *The Apocalypse*, was the first printed work designed and published entirely by one artist. The book told the story of the end of the world with 14 full-page woodcuts like the one described above. Hundreds of copies of the book quickly sold out and spread Dürer's fame throughout Germany. Even the illiterate, the vast majority of the population, could enjoy the book and get the main ideas. What was this thing called printing that could offer so many readers at one time the same terrifying vision?

The kind of printing that enabled Dürer to make many copies of the pictures in *The Apocalypse* had been around for a long time. In fact, the Europeans had been doing it since the twelfth century. They learned it from the Chinese, who had been printing since the eighth century. This kind of printing is called **woodblock printing**. An outline of a picture is cut into a block of wood. Then the rest of the wood is chipped away around the outline, until only the original picture is raised. The block is then inked and pressed onto paper. The printer could make many copies before the wood cracked. This worked well for making images, but it was not practical for pages of words. Not only was it hard to carve the thousands of tiny letters that made up a page of print, but the thousands also had to be cut in reverse.

Because of the difficulty of carving letters, books in the Middle Ages were copied by hand. At first, scribes only had **parchment** to write on. Parchment is made of animal skin, so one copy of the Bible required about 100 calfskins or 300 sheepskins. Remember also that the making of a book would take months because the scribe had to copy all of the pages by hand. The copiest did not just copy the words either. They would often embellish the pages with exquisite, tiny pictures and decorations painted in blue, red, green, and gold. This process is called **illumination**. It is not surprising that books were tremendously expensive and rare. Most books were copied in monasteries, and that is where they tended to stay. Monastery libraries were the best-stocked and would have been proud of a collection of only 500 books.

Eventually, Europeans learned from the Chinese how to make paper from wood pulp. By the fifteenth century, they also learned how to mix ground charcoal and linseed oil to make long-lasting printer's ink. Finally, it was a German goldsmith named Johann Gutenberg who perfected the making of movable metal type. He made models of each letter or character of the alphabet in a hard metal. Using these models, he then made molds of these letters. With the molds, he made unlimited numbers of each letter in molten lead. These lead types, as they are called, could then be set side-by-side in plates that were put together to make a page of print. The plates were then covered with ink and pressed onto paper to make a printed page of text. Gutenberg printed his first pages in this way sometime between 1445 and 1448. When Dürer printed *The Apocalypse* by combining woodblock printing to make pictures with Gutenberg's movable type, the process had already been around for half a century.

Printing had as profound an impact on the Renaissance as the computer has had on today's society. Suddenly many more people had access to much more information. By the year 1500, 40,000 titles had been published, meaning that around nine million individual books were being read. Over half of these were religious books, but next on the list were ancient classics, grammar books, law books, astrology handbooks, encyclopedias, almanacs, and chivalric romances. Printing became a big business, employing thousands of people and involving huge amounts of money.

What resulted from all of this information? A larger part of the population learned to read, and books were more affordable. Education changed because students could read books for themselves and did not have to rely on the lectures of teachers for all of their information. Languages other than Latin or Greek, like English, French, Spanish, and Italian, were standardized. Before printing, these so-called **vernacular** languages had no rules for spelling or punctuation. In fact, they were looked down upon, and only Latin was seen as suitable for respectable writing. With the printing press, literature also emerged rapidly in vernacular languages.

Finally, the printing press spread Renaissance ideas throughout Europe. Through books, more people had access to the ideals of ancient Greece and Rome that had inspired the Renaissance. Other Europeans besides Italians could now learn to look closely at nature and to lead lives dedicated to human growth. More people could perfect their reading of Greek and Latin and take a new and closer look at the main influence of the age, the Bible. Their often drastically different interpretations changed European society forever.

Activities

1. Look at Dürer's *The Four Horsemen* from the Apocalypse Series in *Gardner's Art Through the Ages* by R. G. Tansey and F. S. Kleiner. What does this picture tell you about the imagination and fears of fifteenth-century Germany?

2. Copy a page of a great book by hand. Then illuminate the margins with pictures and decorations. See Renaissance examples of illumination in *The Panorama of the Renaissance* edited by Margaret Aston. (Note: After the invention of the printing press, artists sometimes decorated the margins of a printed page.)

Name _____ Date _____

Challenges

1. Who are the four horsemen in Dürer's print? _____

_____

2. What kind of printing did Dürer use for the artwork in his book? _____

_____

3. Where did Europeans learn to do this kind of printing? _____

_____

4. How many animal skins might go into the making of a Bible? _____

_____

5. Who perfected the making of movable metal type? _____

_____

6. How did the printing press have as profound an impact on the Renaissance as the

computer has had on today's society? _____

_____

7. Give examples of vernacular languages. _____

_____

8. What kinds of books were popular in the sixteenth century? _____

_____

_____

_____

9. How did the printing press help vernacular language? _____

_____

_____

10. How did the printing press spread Renaissance ideas? _____

_____

_____

_____

Name _____ Date _____

Points to Ponder

1. Why did it take Europeans so long to invent the printing press?

_____

_____

_____

_____

_____

2. What does the subject matter of Dürer's book tell you about what interested sixteenth-century readers?

_____

_____

_____

_____

_____

3. How is information power?

_____

_____

_____

_____

_____

The Reformation

Martin Luther

As Martin Luther trotted away from the city, the late afternoon sun cast long shadows beneath his horse's feet. Ahead of him, the forest was already somber and ominous. As the road took its last curve around a ruined cottage, he could see nothing before him. He rode on, all his senses awake to the strange sounds and black shapes around him. If his enemies wished him harm, here was the place to do it. Then, to his horror, he saw large, dark shapes moving toward him. He wheeled his horse around to escape and saw more shapes coming at him from behind. Out of the darkness came a rough, military voice. "Dr. Luther, we have been sent by the duke of Saxony. We are to escort you to the duke's castle, for your protection. You have many enemies, Doctor, but you can count the duke as a friend."

Luther did have many enemies, and it is not surprising. In 1517, this professor from the University of Wittenburg posted his 95 theses on the door of the Wittenburg Church. He wanted to debate about the sale of indulgences, and the 95 theses were his key arguments. **Indulgences** were documents sold by the church that were supposed to lessen the punishment for sinners in the afterlife. Luther's 95 theses were quickly published and distributed throughout Germany due to the newly invented printing presses. This caused an unforeseen explosion of complaints against the church.

The church in the early sixteenth century was different from what we know today. All Europeans belonged to one Christian church (the Roman Catholic church). The church was ruled over by bishops, archbishops, cardinals, and, at the top, the Pope in Rome. Almost a quarter of all farmland in Europe was owned by the church, so it was wealthy and influential. Priests were well-paid, but they were exempt from taxation. The **clergy**, as all of these churchmen were called, even had their own laws and law courts that were separate from the rest of the population. They also enjoyed the advantage of being one of the few groups of people in the sixteenth century who knew how to read and write. All of this, in addition to the fact that religion was at the center of people's lives, made the clergy the most powerful group in Europe.

With such a large and powerful human organization, there were bound to be problems. Some people felt the church was too preoccupied with money. Others criticized the church for getting too involved in politics. Still others felt that the church was controlled by Italians and no one else. When Luther condemned the sale of indulgences, others quickly followed his lead and began criticizing the church in other ways. The motives of the critics were mixed. For instance, German princes supported Luther because they hoped to seize church property. However, other thinking men and women, like Luther, genuinely wanted to improve religious life in Europe.

The Pope, Leo X, feared that Luther would weaken the church. Therefore, he tried to silence him. Luther was called to defend himself before a council of princes, bishops, and cardinals. Instead of giving in, he only added to his list of recommendations for reform. Fortunately, Luther had powerful friends, or he might have been arrested and executed. The duke of Saxony, as we saw above, gave him protection in his castle, the Wartburg. While hiding in the Wartburg, Luther used his time to translate the New Testament of the Bible from Latin into German. This activity grew out of one of Luther's main beliefs, that all people should be able to read the Bible for themselves. The publication of this book laid the foundation for the modern German language.

Because of the printing press, Luther's ideas about how the church should change spread throughout Europe. As a result, within a decade the church was permanently split in two. The followers of Luther's ideas came to be called **Protestants**. In an age when religion was taken so seriously, such an event was bound to have dramatic consequences. In Germany, peasants thought to themselves, if Luther could challenge the authority of the church, why couldn't they defy the authority of their landlords? In 1524, a revolt broke out. It was crushed, but only after countless peasants were killed. Meanwhile, princes and kings made themselves more wealthy by seizing church property. The question of religion also found its way into relations between kingdoms. For the next 130 years, Europe was torn apart by warfare as Protestants and Catholics battled for power. Even within the Protestant church, divisions began to occur. John Calvin broke away from the Lutherans and founded Calvinism. Conrad Grebel separated from other Protestants and founded the Anabaptists.

Although many left the old church to join the Protestant churches, the majority of Europeans remained faithful to the Catholic tradition. They still preferred the rituals and ceremonies and admired the way the old church cared for the poor and sick. However, many Catholics admitted there was a need for reform. The leaders of the Catholic church finally met in the Italian city of Trent in 1545 to decide if the break with the Protestants could be healed. The Council of Trent put through many reforms. For instance, it insisted upon better education for priests, less preoccupation with wealth, and the end of the sale of indulgences. However, on other important matters, it reaffirmed basic beliefs that the church had held before Luther published his 95 theses. Priests, for instance, were still seen as the main interpreters of the Bible. Luther believed that anyone could interpret the Bible for him- or herself. Much of modern Catholicism grew out of the Council of Trent. At the same time, the council was unable to reach an agreement with the Protestants, and religion in Europe remained permanently divided.

Activities

1. Draw a set of cartoons highlighting the abuses of the church in the sixteenth century. (A good place to look for examples of sixteenth-century woodblock prints that do this is *Here I Stand, A Life of Martin Luther* by R. H. Bainton.)

2. Look at selections of Luther's 95 theses in the book mentioned above. What were Luther's main complaints?

Name _____ Date _____

Challenges

1. What was the purpose of Luther's 95 theses? _____

_____

_____

2. What were indulgences? _____

_____

3. How was the church in the early fifteenth century different from today? _____

_____

4. What advantages did the clergy enjoy?_____

_____

_____

_____

5. What were the main criticisms of the church? _____

_____

_____

6. What were some of the motives of the church's critics? _____

_____

7. What did Luther do while hiding in the Wartburg? _____

_____

8. What caused the Peasants' Revolt? _____

_____

9. Why did many Europeans remain faithful to the old church? _____

_____

10. How did the Council of Trent reform the old church? _____

_____

_____

Name _____ Date _____

Points to Ponder

1. Why are people, both in the sixteenth century and today, prepared to go to war over religious differences?

_____

_____

_____

_____

_____

2. Why were political leaders in the sixteenth century so jealous of the church's power?

_____

_____

_____

_____

_____

3. How did the Renaissance cause the Reformation?

_____

_____

_____

_____

_____

Music and the Harmony of the Spheres

"I believe music unfit for soldiers," announced Lord Gaspar, striking a martial pose.

"With all due respect, my friend, you are very wrong," said the Count.

"But what could music possibly offer me?" snorted Lord Gaspar.

"Let me remind you," replied the Count, "that the Greek philosopher, Pythagoras, said that the world is made of music. The planets and the stars move according to the rules of harmony and melody. Plato himself agreed and said that music spoke directly to the deepest part of the soul. Therefore, harmonious and melodic music is necessary to make healthy and sane people."

"Oh, very fine words, Count, but I can see nothing in them but hot air," replied Lord Gaspar. "I can neither sing nor play, and I am none the worse for it." And with that, Lord Gaspar strode over to a less taxing discussion taking place in the corner about boar hunting.

Chuckling, the Count turned to his companions and shrugged his shoulders. "When example is at hand, what need is there for words?"

The dialogue above is based on similar conversations that can be found in the sixteenth-century best seller, *The Courtier*, by Baldisarre Castiglione. It was a guidebook for how to succeed in Renaissance upper-class society. It also created a model for what the ideal Renaissance man or woman should be. The sixteenth-century readers would have agreed wholeheartedly with Castiglione's emphasis upon music, because they saw its positive effects all around them. Music was enjoyed by a larger segment of the population than any of the other arts. Peasants in the fields sang folk songs to help pass their long, dreary days. At weddings, the bagpipe or hurdy gurdy, the two most popular instruments of the countryside, supplied raucous music for dance and merriment. On the other end of the social scale, the ability to sing and play at least one musical instrument was seen as an important skill by the upper classes. Lutes, viols, flutes, and harps were popular instruments. Often, supper was followed by an evening of musical performance. Sometimes music was even printed on large sheets placed in the center of a table so that guests sitting around the table would know their parts. No doubt, guests like Lord Gaspar above were an embarrassment.

Innovation is part of the story of Renaissance music, just as it is in art, literature, science, and technology. Renaissance thinkers believed that music had reached perfection in ancient Greece. Although almost no ancient music survived, books about ancient music theory did, and Renaissance composers used them to write their own music. This meant that music was written according to mathematical laws, which the ancients believed linked

54

the universe together. Only through the understanding of what was thought to be the purest of all languages, mathematics, could Renaissance composers write music that harmonized with the planets.

It was in Flanders, instead of Italy, that early Renaissance music flourished. There, composers created complex harmonies and polyphony. **Polyphony** is music written for more than one voice. The voices sing separate parts, but they harmonize to create chords. This was different from late medieval music, which, though beautiful, could be discordant and emphasized a single line of notes with a minimum of polyphony. In the place of the single line, the composers of Renaissance Flanders created a stream of ever-shifting chords. Listening to Renaissance polyphony requires the listener to abandon any search for a melody and just float in the effusion of harmony.

Like other northern Europeans, Flemish composers and musicians were drawn to Renaissance Italy. In Italian city-states, they found wealthy, open-minded patrons who were willing to pay for creative new compositions. For example, Lorenzo de' Medici of Florence persuaded the composer Heinrich Isaac of Flanders to be court composer and tutor his children. In Italy, Isaac and other Flemish composers were also influenced by the Renaissance humanists' love of language. They reacted against the tendency in medieval music to focus on the notes, which caused the listener to miss the lyrics. The new music of the fifteenth century was written in such a way that the words were clearly sung and the music reflected their meaning. All of these factors came together to produce profoundly beautiful polyphonic choral music. Because religion was at the center of European life, many of the choral compositions in the fifteenth century were religious in nature. The two most common types of compositions were **masses** and **motets**, which were religious texts put to music for church services.

At the same time, choral music was written for activities not related to church, like festivals, weddings, courtship, and entertainment. The word we use to describe such activities is **secular**. The most popular form of this secular music was the **madrigal**. Initially, a madrigal was an Italian poem set to music for two or more voices. The subject matter of these songs then, as now, was romantic love. By the end of the sixteenth century, more secular music was being written than religious.

Along with choral music, instrumental music also developed. In the Middle Ages, instrumental music was considered less important than choral music. As a result, little from the Middle Ages has survived, though it was widely performed. In the Renaissance, instrumental music began to be taken seriously, and well-regarded composers wrote music just for groups of instruments. The most popular household instrument was the **lute**. This was a pear-shaped string instrument. It had one single string and five double strings with a neck fretted like a guitar. The most common wind instruments were recorders, but there were many others, with funny names like shawm, crummhorn, korthold, rauschpfeife, and sackbut. Social upper classes were expected to know the many complex dance steps of the day, which had names like Pavane, Galliard, and Allemande. To accommodate this passion for dance, a great deal of instrumental music was written.

Music of all types was made more available because many copies could be printed on the printing press. This helped to spread the new innovations in music throughout Europe. Truly, the Renaissance world was moving to the harmony of the spheres.

Name _____ Date _____

Challenges

1. What did the Greek philosopher Pythagoras say about music? _____

_____

_____

2. Who wrote a guidebook for how to succeed in the Renaissance world? _____

_____

3. What were the two most popular instruments of the countryside? _____

_____

4. What were the most popular instruments of the upper classes? _____

_____

5. According to Renaissance thinkers, when had music reached perfection? _____

_____

6. Where were most of the great composers from in the fifteenth century? _____

_____

7. Who employed Heinrich Isaac as court composer and tutor? _____

_____

8. What impact did the humanists have on music? _____

_____

_____

9. What was a madrigal? _____

_____

10. What invention helped spread musical innovation throughout Europe? _____

_____

Name _____ Date _____

Points to Ponder

1. Do you agree with Plato that music speaks directly to the deepest part of the soul? Explain your answer.

_____

_____

_____

_____

_____

2. How were Renaissance ideas about music similar to Renaissance ideas about art?

_____

_____

_____

_____

_____

3. If the Renaissance world moved to the harmony of the spheres, to what does the modern world move? Explain your answer.

_____

_____

_____

_____

_____

Name _____ Date _____

Activities

1. Listen to some Renaissance polyphony. Recordings of works by Renaissance composers Giovanni Pierluigi da Palestrina, Thomas Tallis, Orlando Lassus, Josquin, and Heinrich Isaac are easy to find. Two good recordings are *Florentine Carnival, Festival Music for Lorenzo de' Medici* by the London Pro-Musica, directed by Bernard Thomas, and *Beyond Chant* by the Voices of Ascension, directed by Dennis Keene.

2. Recordings of Renaissance dance music are also easy to find. Two good recordings are *Dances from Terpsichore* by the Ulsamer Collegium and the Collegium Terpsichore, directed by Siegfried Behrend and Giegried Fink, and *Watkins Ale* by the Baltimore Consort. Once you have located some Renaissance dance music, try doing the Pavane, one of the simplest and most popular dances of the age.

   The Pavane is slow and should be danced with grace and poise. It is a processional and dancers move in a circular pattern.

   1. At the beginning of the Pavane, musicians play the last few measures of the tune. This is for the Honor or Reverence. When you hear this, gentlemen slide the right foot back, bend the right leg, and remove the hat with the left hand. Ladies do the same but do not move the right foot as far or remove the hat.

   2. Once the Reverence is over, partners stand side by side with women on the right. With elbow bent and palm down, the gentleman holds his arm horizontally to the ground. The lady places her arm upon it.

   3. Begin the dance with the left foot. Land on the ball of the foot as if tip-toeing.

   4. Next, close with the right foot in the same way. As you close, lower your heels.

   5. Do the same as above, leading with the right foot this time.

   6. Take a regular step with your left foot.

   7. Take a regular step with your right foot.

   8. Then begin the pattern again by stepping with the left foot.

   9. At the end of the dance, the musicians will hold the last note for a final Reverence.

   For other dances, see *Daily Life in Elizabethan England* by J. L. Singman.

Food, Feasts, and Manners

With a thunderous roll of drums and blare of trumpets, into the great hall came the food. It started with a cooked peacock, prepared so that its magnificent feathers were fully displayed. The guests oohed and aahed. Next came a huge pie filled with live, singing birds. Immediately after this was a roast swan, decorated with red and gold candied fruits. A succession of other dishes, equally spectacular, followed. Finally, the end of what was just the first course was marked by the arrival of the **cockentrice**. This mythical animal was created by sewing the upper part of a baked chicken to the lower part of a roasted pig. Amid laughter and lively conversation, the guests began to feast.

Eating in the Renaissance could be as much spectacle as sustenance. The dishes mentioned above could easily have been eaten by the wealthy at special occasions, of which the Renaissance had many. There were births, baptisms, weddings, funerals, victory celebrations, both diplomatic and military, and a score of religious feasts throughout the year. These included Christmas, but also Epiphany on January 6, Candelmas on February 2, Whitsunday on May 3, Holy Rood Day on September 14, Michelmas on September 29, and All Saints Day on November 1, to name only a few.

As you can see above, the word *course* meant something different in the Renaissance than it does today. There were usually three courses, but a meal could have as many as 17. Each course could include as many as 15 different dishes. What might these dishes be? It was always important to have a few like the dishes described for theatrical effect. Then, to accompany these, there might be salmon belly, roast porpoise and peas, baked herring with sugar, or baked pheasant with cold herb jelly. For vegetables, there could be lemon rice with almonds, fried squash flowers, or artichokes with blueberry rice. This could be followed by parsnip and apple fritters, figs stuffed with cinnamoned eggs, and Elderberry funnel cakes.

A course could last for hours and would be accompanied or interspersed with music and entertainment. Sometimes jugglers or acrobats were served in enormous puddings and would leap out to astonish guests. Then there were the jesters, dwarfs, and wildmen. There would also be an orchestra. For example, the d'Este family, who ruled the city of Ferrara, entertained guests at one of their feasts with six singers, six viols, a lute, a trombone, a recorder, a flute, and a keyboard instrument. In many instances, guests were treated to a theatrical performance after the meal.

Italian theater at the time was done in a style that is called **Commedia dell' arte**. The Commedia troupes did slapstick comedies. In fact, our modern word *slapstick* comes from the name of a Commedia prop used to hit actors for a laugh. Traveling troupes of actors would dress in masks and stylized costumes. This was so the audiences would recognize the characters. All Commedia dell' arte shows used the same characters. There was Harlequino, who always wore patchwork quilts and played the clever servant. Then there was Pantalone, the foolish old father who could be recognized by his huge pants. Then there was the swaggering, bragging II Capitano, with his long sword that was always getting stuck in its scabbard. Most Commedia characters had a collection of jokes and skits they used as needed in different performances.

The guests at a banquet enjoyed the food and entertainment immensely, but there were definite rules about etiquette and table manners. Spoons were used for soups and puddings and knives were used for meat, of which there was always a great deal. However, all else was eaten with hands. Certain fingers were extended while eating specific foods to allow clean fingertips to be ready for the next dish. Many dishes in the Renaissance were designed specifically to be eaten with the hands. Breads, pies, and pastries filled with meat, fish, or fruit were common dishes for this reason. Nevertheless, Renaissance cuisine used plenty of sauces, gravies, stuffings, and cream, so skill was required to eat gracefully. Fingers were washed in bowls of lemon-scented water between courses and at the end of a meal.

Renaissance table manners may have been less refined than what we are used to today. Giovanni della Casa, the author of a guidebook on good manners, suggested the following to his readers: Do not clean your teeth with your napkin. It is impolite to scratch yourself at the table. You should avoid spitting at mealtimes, but if you must, then do so in a decent manner. You should not carry toothpicks behind your ears, and you should not make nasty noises with your lips. Finally, he reminded his readers, when blowing your nose, you should not open the handkerchief and inspect it, as if pearls or rubies had dropped out.

Name _____ Date _____

Challenges

1. What was a cockentrice? _____

_____

2. List three religious feast days. _____

_____

3. How many courses might there be in a Renaissance feast? _____

_____

4. List three dishes that might have been served at a feast. _____

_____

5. What kinds of plays did the Commedia dell' arte do? _____

_____

6. What was the slapstick? _____

_____

7. List three Commedia dell' arte characters. _____

_____

_____

8. Because most food was eaten by hand, what kinds of dishes were popular? _____

_____

9. How did guests at a feast keep their fingers clean? _____

_____

_____

10. List two examples of bad manners. _____

_____

_____

Name _____ Date _____

Points to Ponder

1. How is Renaissance food different from today's food?

_____

_____

_____

_____

_____

2 Why do you think hosts were willing to spend so much money on feasts?

_____

_____

_____

_____

_____

3. How do table manners today compare with table manners in the Renaissance?

_____

_____

_____

_____

_____

Name _____ Date _____

Activities

1. Most Commedia dell' arte performances used the same basic story line. The rest was improvised by the actors. The story went as follows: A foolish old father wants his daughter to marry an older man for money. However, the daughter is in love with someone else her own age. A clever servant helps the young couple trick the father into allowing them to marry, and they live happily ever after. Using that plot outline, write a Commedia dell' arte style skit.

2. Cook this Renaissance appetizer called Amondyn Eyroun. (This recipe is taken from *Fabulous Feasts* by M. P. Cosman.)

   Ingredients:
   - 1 cup ricotta cheese
   - 8 Tablespoons butter
   - $\frac{3}{4}$ cup slivered or coarsely ground almonds
   - $\frac{2}{3}$ cup oats
   - 4 hard-boiled eggs, chopped
   - $\frac{1}{2}$ cup softened raisins
   - 6 raw eggs
   - 2 Tablespoons honey
   - $\frac{1}{2}$ teaspoon fennel seed, crushed
   - 2 Tablespoons oil for sautéing

   Method:
   1. Place ricotta in a large bowl.
   2. In a large, heavy skillet, melt half of the butter; toast the almonds and oats until golden. Pour off almonds, oats, and butter into the ricotta and mix well. Reserve skillet, and any residual butter therein, for later.
   3. Stir chopped hard-boiled eggs and raisins into the ricotta mixture.
   4. Beat the raw eggs with honey, salt, and fennel.
   5. Stir the sweetened eggs into the cheese mixture.
   6. Heat remaining butter with oil in skillet. Pour mixture in to fry until golden, about 5 to 8 minutes on very low heat. Turn the omelette if you prefer the eggs well done. Cut into individual wedges and serve hot.

Fashion and Hygiene

Imagine yourself, recently arrived in Florence and out for a stroll in the early evening of a warm, Italian summer. The year is 1465. What would you expect to see? Most of the streets that you would walk through would be narrow and crowded by the red-tiled apartments and shops of the ordinary Florentines. In the wealthier parts of town, you would see recently built churches and palaces with columns, arches, and proportions modeled on classical Greek and Roman architecture. Of course, in addition to buildings, you would also see the people who inhabited these structures. What would they look like?

One of the first things you would notice when encountering a typical wealthy woman of the Renaissance would be her high, dome-like forehead. She would have plucked her hair to halfway across her head. The eyelashes, along with most of the eyebrows, would also be plucked out. Her hair would be bleached blond by spending hours every day in the sun, under a wide-brimmed sunhat without a crown. It would then be washed with lemon juice and brushed with sulfur. White and gold braid with rubies or sapphires would decorate her tresses. The woman would also have a white complexion, because suntans were only appropriate for peasant women. To enhance the whiteness of her skin, she would have used cosmetics made of mercury, pearls, silver, or egg shells. You might be surprised at how wooden and silent she appears. The reason for this could well be that the thickness of her face paint prevents her from smiling or talking. In addition to the face, there would be cosmetics on her neck and hands. Cheeks, ears, and fingertips would be touched with rouge to give the impression of health.

**A fashionable Italian couple
of the Renaissance period**

This typical woman of wealth might be dressed in a loose-fitting, high-waisted brocade gown that hung to the floor, sleeves embroidered in gold and masses of pearls around the neck. When walking in the street, she would wear clogs that raised her six inches off the ground and kept her gown out of the mud. She may or may not have fit the ideal Renaissance body type of plumpness. If she had the misfortune to be thin, she may well have resorted to special high-calorie medicines in order to avoid losing weight.

Men's fashions were similarly grand. First of all, whiteness was associated with the feminine, so a man would blacken his beard with dye. He would also wear tight, multi-colored hose and no pants. Over this, you would see a short upper garment called a **doublet** or **jerkin**. This garment would have detachable slashed sleeves so the white shirt underneath could be seen. Since buttons and zippers were not yet in use, it was closed with many tiny hooks and rings called **points**. On his belt, you would see a dagger, and on his

64

feet, you would see the latest of fashion, square-toed shoes. Hair was worn shoulder length underneath a flat, felt cap. Around his neck, you might see a chain with a jeweled pendant.

In the Renaissance, bathing was no longer popular, so a variety of smells would have greeted you on your walk. In the Middle Ages, public baths had been common. However, in the Renaissance, the medical profession began to believe that one was more likely to catch diseases when bathing. They thought that open pores would allow the body's vital forces to escape. Nevertheless, fewer baths did not mean that people looked or smelled worse than before, just different. In fact, appearance in the Renaissance was more important than it had ever been. Appearance, like manners, became a way for the upper classes to mark themselves off from those below them. Water was replaced with so-called dry ways of cleaning. Powder was used as a sort of dry shampoo that was left on the head overnight and then combed out in the morning. Scented towels were used to rub the face and torso. Heavy doses of perfumes were sprinkled on clothing and furniture. People in the lower classes could not afford powder or perfumes and either resorted to bathing or remained filthy.

Wealthy people during the Renaissance believed very strongly in the importance of changing clothes, in particular the linen undergarments. In fact, bathing was no longer considered a necessity because it was believed that fresh linens kept people cleaner than bathing. Of course, the use of linen, like everything else in the Renaissance, depended upon social class. Most workers or artisans wore shirts made of hemp, which cost about one-fourth as much as a linen undergarment. Their outer garments might also be of hemp or wool. The same was true of ordinary women in the city or countryside.

Fashion changed almost as often as the weather. What was true of the 1460s was already out of fashion in the 1470s. People have always valued appearance and staying abreast of changing styles. The same was true of the Renaissance, but more so. Wealthy Renaissance men and women wanted to show that they were different from those below them. They did this by adopting cultivated manners and classical education. Ever more costly and elaborate fashions, however, were an easier way for the rich to display their social standing.

Activities

1. Look at Raphael's *Marriage of the Virgin* or *Madonna with the Goldfinch*. Then look at Leonardo da Vinci's *Mona Lisa* and *Virgin of the Rocks*. (All of these works can be found in *Gardner's Art Through the Ages* by R. G. Tansey and F. S. Kleiner.) Compare the Renaissance ideal of feminine beauty revealed in these works with that found in a modern fashion magazine.

2. Using the description of men's and women's fashions found in the chapter and any paintings from the Renaissance that you have studied, draw a portrait of a fashion-conscious couple of the fifteenth century.

Name _____ Date _____

Challenges

1. Why did Renaissance women have dome-like foreheads? _____

_____

2. Why did ladies want to avoid suntans? _____

_____

3. What were cosmetics made from? _____

_____

_____

4. What do you call the short upper garment worn by men? _____

_____

5. Without buttons or zippers, how was clothing kept closed? _____

_____

6. Why were Renaissance physicians opposed to bathing? _____

_____

_____

7. Why was appearance so important in the Renaissance? _____

_____

_____

8. Give an example of a dry way of cleaning. _____

_____

_____

9. What kinds of materials were undergarments made from? _____

_____

10. Why was clean linen so important? _____

_____

_____

Name _____ Date _____

Points to Ponder

1. Why were the upper classes in the Renaissance so determined to mark themselves off from the lower classes?

_____

_____

_____

_____

_____

2. What popular fashions today do you think will appear ridiculous in the future?

_____

_____

_____

_____

_____

3. Where does fashion come from?

_____

_____

_____

_____

_____

A New Way of Looking at the Universe

A Renaissance scholar

If you were an educated person at the beginning of the sixteenth century, you would have believed that the universe was shaped like an onion. You would have held a **geocentric** view of the universe. That is, you would have believed that the earth was at the center of all things and surrounding it were layers of revolving transparent substances in the shape of spheres. Stuck into these layers of invisible material were the Sun, the Moon, the planets, and the stars. Because you would have believed that motion was unnatural, you would suspect that the planets and the stars were being pushed by angels. This was the universe of Ptolemy, a Greek astronomer and geographer who had lived almost 1,300 years before the Renaissance. Ptolemy remained the most important authority on astronomy in the early sixteenth century. However, this orderly picture of the universe was about to be challenged.

In the Middle Ages, people relied on religion to answer questions about the meaning of life and people's relationship to nature. Religion, however, offered little on day-to-day physical matters like how to increase the speed of ships, how to fire cannons more accurately, or how to cure disease. Behind these kinds of questions was the big question: "How is the physical world structured?". For the answers to concrete problems in nature, Europeans relied on three major traditions.

The first tradition was the one practiced by artisans and engineers. It was their job to find practical solutions to ordinary problems. Blacksmiths worked at improving horseshoes and swords. Engineers erected dams and built roads. Together they invented windmills and plows. By the sixteenth century, these men had attained a down-to-earth understanding of the way nature operated. Sometimes they could even control it. The bigger picture, however, was left to somebody else.

The second tradition was that of the magicians. They could be found at all levels of society. So-called "wise" men and women in villages used omens, herbs, and spells to explain the works of nature, and they tried to control it by these means. In the cities, learned **alchemists** experimented with strange liquids, powders, animal parts, and metals to unlock the secrets of the universe. They sought to control nature by turning one element into another. They also experimented in curing wounds and sickness. Others called **astrologers** sought to understand the future by reading secrets revealed in the stars. Although these magicians went about practicing their arts in different ways, they all believed that nature was organized in regular, predictable structures. If one could discover those underlying structures, then one could command the universe!

The third tradition was practiced by the natural philosophers. These men could be found mainly in universities. Here, it was believed that the nature of the universe was

68

revealed in ancient books. Their favorite author was Aristotle. They also read Ptolemy's works on geography and astronomy and Galen's writings on medicine. The Renaissance interest in ancient languages and books added to the natural philosophers' understanding of these authorities. By the sixteenth century, scholars had already begun to graft new ideas onto older theories. For example, Renaissance map-makers used Ptolemy's ideas to make their own maps of the world, much of which Ptolemy had never known.

In the sixteenth century, these three traditions began to come together due to the printing press and the rising interest in the natural world. A good example of the results can be seen in the ideas of Nicholas Copernicus (1473–1543). He was perplexed because Ptolemy's geocentric view of the universe did not always explain the observed movements of the planets. For instance, at times the planets appeared to be moving backwards around the earth. Nothing in Ptolemy's theory would explain this. Copernicus solved the problem by proposing a radical solution. In 1543, he published a book entitled *On the Revolution of the Celestial Spheres,* which argued that the Sun was in the center of the solar system, not the earth. This is a **heliocentric** or Sun-centered view. He said that the earth and other celestial bodies were in constant motion around the Sun. Copernicus provided a more consistent explanation of the planets' movements than did Ptolemy. As widely held as this view became, it would be almost a century before Copernicus's theory was proven. However, this Polish astronomer inspired a new generation to observe the night sky differently.

Another pioneer in modern science was an alchemist known as Doctor Paracelsus (1493–1541). He realized that knowledge about the human body came only from close observation and experimentation. His studies led him to reject the early sixteenth-century notion of the four humors. The humors were believed to be the four main fluids in the body: **blood**, **phlegm**, and **red and black bile**. (They were also know as hot, cold, wet, and dry.) Most medical doctors at the time believed that health was maintained by keeping the four humors in balance. The common practice of **bloodletting**, which involved draining controlled amounts of blood from the body, was intended to correct an imbalance of the humors. An individual's horoscope at the time of birth was also thought to influence one's balance of humors. Therefore, astrologers were as important as medical doctors in achieving cures. Paracelsus' experimental methods led him to believe that an illness could be treated and cured with medicine designed for just that illness. As a result, he laid the foundation for the use of modern medicine.

Other pioneers followed Copernicus and Paracelsus as the practice of modern science continued to develop in the sixteenth century. By the mid 1500s, three central characteristics of modern science were widely accepted. First, it was important to be boundlessly curious. Second, a scientist should reject old assumptions and methods unless they could be proven as true. Third, the way to test ideas was through experimentation and careful observation. Because the important discoveries during these years were so radical, historians call these developments the Scientific Revolution.

Activities

1. Write a skit in which representatives of the three major traditions debate about the nature of the physical world.
2. Draw a map of Ptolemy's view of the universe (for good sixteenth-century examples, see *The Panorama of the Renaissance* edited by M. Aston.)

Name _____ Date _____

Challenges

1. If you believed in the geocentric view of the universe, what was the center of the universe?

_____

2. How did the geocentric view explain the movement of the planets and stars? _____

_____

_____

3. What was the job of blacksmiths and engineers? _____

_____

_____

4. What would a person who mixed goat tongues with herbs and lead in order to discover

the secrets of the universe be called? _____

_____

5. What was a person called who tried to understand the future by reading the stars?

_____

6. What group was most interested in the work of Aristotle, Ptolemy, and Galen?

_____

7. What is the center of the universe according to the heliocentric view? _____

_____

8. What were the four humors? _____

_____

9. How did Paracelsus think disease was cured? _____

_____

_____

10. What do historians call the new attitudes toward observation and experimentation that

became popular in the sixteenth century? _____

_____

Name _____ Date _____

Points to Consider

1. Which of the three major traditions seemed the closest to the truth?

_____

_____

_____

_____

_____

2. If you had held a geocentric view of the universe before, how would Copernicus's ideas change the way you felt when looking at the night sky?

_____

_____

_____

_____

_____

3. Why were the three central characteristics of modern science mentioned in the last paragraph so significant?

_____

_____

_____

_____

_____

The Age of Exploration

The Monopode is a one-legged man whose foot is so large that it can be used as a parasol against the hot sun. The Blemmye has no head, but his eyes, nose, and mouth are in the middle of his chest. Thus wrote Sir John Mandeville, describing the supposed inhabitants of unexplored lands in one of the best-selling books of the fourteenth century. The curiosity of the Renaissance in the fifteenth century meant that these legends were soon discarded and replaced by something closer to the truth. At the end of the fifteenth century, dozens of expeditions sailed into unknown waters and dramatically transformed the lives of Europeans and those they encountered forever.

A caravel

In 1487, Bartholomeu Dias of Portugal was the first-known European explorer to round the southern tip of Africa and enter the Indian Ocean. Then, in 1497, Vasco Da Gama, another sea captain working for the King of Portugal, pushed farther into uncharted waters. Sailing around the southern tip of Africa and across the Indian Ocean, he reached India. Meanwhile, an Italian from Genoa named Christopher Columbus persuaded Isabella, the Queen of Spain, to finance an expedition headed due west into the Atlantic. The stories that he brought back inspired others to follow his lead and explore both North and South America, continents unimagined by Europeans before Columbus. Remarkably, for every ship that returned laden with wonder and wealth, another lay at the bottom of the sea. What could have prompted individuals in the late fifteenth century to take such risks with their money and their lives?

There were many reasons why the great age of exploration came about. First, knowledge about the world beyond Europe had been growing for centuries. Most educated people in the fifteenth century knew that the world was round. One of the main sources of this geographical knowledge was the second-century writer, Ptolemy. He advised his readers to draw maps that reflected the way the world looks, not the way they wanted it to look. Ptolemy was discovered again by Renaissance scholars in 1410. Thereafter, his influence spread. **Topographers**, or map-makers, began to correct the medieval notion that Jerusalem was the center of the universe. Another influence was the traveler, Marco Polo. He had gone with his father and uncle to China in 1271. There he made friends with the ruler, Kublai Khan, and became a wealthy man. Realizing that China could become dangerous for him when Kublai Khan died, Polo took advantage of an opportunity to leave. He escorted the Khan's sister to Persia by way of Sumatra and India. When he returned to Venice, Polo wrote about his adventures, the places he had been, and the wealth he had seen. With the invention of the printing press in 1445, maps and travel books like Marco Polo's were suddenly available to more readers than ever before. It is not surprising that readers like Christopher Columbus were stirred into action.

Another important reason for exploration was trade. Over the centuries, Europeans had gradually developed a taste for luxury items from China, India, and Southeast Asia. The city-state of Venice acquired wealth and established a monopoly thanks to its role as middle-man between Europe and Asia. Venetians channeled cottons, silks, taffeta, muslin, damask, dye-stuffs, medicines, spices, perfumes, and pearls into Europe at great profit. Sometimes the merchants of Venice inflated prices as much as 2,000 percent. Oddly enough, European buyers had little knowledge of where these objects came from, but they knew they wanted more. The only thing they were certain of was that a place called Asia was the source of that which was most beautiful, luxurious, and delicious. If they could break the Venetian monopoly on trade and establish direct contact with the Orient, then they could lower purchasing costs to themselves and increase their profits.

The same ambition that propelled the Portuguese explorers Dias and Da Gama drove the Queen of Spain to finance Columbus' search for an Atlantic route to the Orient. Wishful thinking led Columbus and others who followed him into believing that the coasts of North and South America were the Asian mainland.

A third motivation for exploration was religion. Christian Europe during the Renaissance felt besieged by Islamic warriors from the Middle East and North Africa. War between the followers of the two religions had been waging for four centuries. Beginning in 1095, this conflict caused thousands of Christian soldiers from all over Europe to gather into huge armies that repeatedly invaded the Middle East. These many invasions are referred to as the **Crusades**. By the fifteenth century, the tide had turned, and Moslem warriors had successfully conquered much of eastern Europe. Christian Europe felt threatened and sought new allies. Many believed in the legend of an incredibly rich, Christian king named Prester John, who lived in Africa or Asia. Explorers hoped to make contact with Prester John and enlist his help in attacking the Moslem invaders from the flank. Despite the fact that this mythical king was never located, religiously motivated exploration continued. Conversion of unknown people ignorant of Christianity became a primary focus.

Finally, new kinds of ships and rigging made sailing the open seas less dangerous. In the fifteenth century, the Portuguese designed a ship called the **caravel**, which was more suitable for sailing on the high seas. It had a hinged rudder, deep-draft hulls, and a new combination of square and triangular sails. These improvements allowed explorers to sail in all kinds of wind. The discovery of the **astrolabe** enabled sailors to calculate their latitude by establishing the position of the Sun and stars. Magnetic compasses helped them keep track of direction. With improved ships and new navigational devices, sailors could brave the unknown Atlantic.

In the fifteenth and sixteenth centuries, the European encounter with previously unknown lands and people was as dramatic to them as the discovery of a populated planet would be to us today. Explorers learned things about the world that even Sir John Mandeville could not have invented.

Activities

1. Write a proposal to the Queen of Spain in which you try to persuade her to finance your expedition in search of a new route to Asia. Remember to include arguments that you think will be most persuasive to a sixteenth-century ruler.
2. Look at some of the fifteenth- and sixteenth-century maps found in *New Worlds, Ancient Texts* by A. Grafton or *The Panorama of the Renaissance* edited by M. Aston. Using the old maps as models, draw your own version of the New World as it would have been seen in the sixteenth century.

Name _____ Date _____

Challenges

1. What new inventions made the sea safer for sailors? _____

_____

_____

2. Who was the first European explorer to sail around the southern tip of Africa?

_____

3. Who was the main source for geographical knowledge? _____

_____

4. Where did Marco Polo's travels take him? _____

_____

_____

5. What Italian city benefited most from trade with the East? _____

_____

6. What was Columbus searching for? _____

_____

7. What items did the Europeans want from the East? _____

_____

_____

8. Who threatened Christian Europe in the fifteenth century? _____

_____

9. What are the many invasions of the Middle East by Christian warriors called?

_____

10. What was the name of the mythical Christian king who was supposed to live in Africa?

_____

Name _____ Date _____

Points to Ponder

1. How was the European encounter with North and South America like the discovery of a new, populated planet would be today?

_____

_____

_____

_____

_____

_____

2. Which of the reasons for the age of exploration do you think are the most important?

_____

_____

_____

_____

_____

_____

3. How does the motivation for exploration help to explain the way native Americans were treated by explorers?

_____

_____

_____

_____

_____

_____

Power: The Rise of the Nation-State and Machiavelli

Niccolo Machiavelli

"Is it better for a prince to be loved more than feared or feared more than loved? The answer is that he should be both, but since it is difficult to be feared and loved at the same time, it is much safer to be feared." These lines were written by Niccolo Machiavelli in his handbook for politicians called *The Prince*. He wrote other similarly disturbing suggestions: Humans will more quickly forgive the killing of a family member than having property taken from them. Often, for the good of the community, people must suffer. A prince who is too merciful will be judged weak, so he should get used to the necessity of causing pain. The prince must learn to lie and cheat for the good of his subjects and recognize that he is above the laws he uses to govern others. In other words, the ends justify the means.

Machiavelli's writings have often been judged as evil. However, he would have claimed that he was only giving practical advice based on his first-hand political experience. Politics was a dangerous game when he wrote his book in 1513. Rulers during the Renaissance were more likely to die violently on the battlefield or by the hands of an assassin than peacefully in their beds. Machiavelli's diplomatic career put him in a position to observe this cut-throat world.

The government of Florence employed Machiavelli as an ambassador and sent him on 24 diplomatic missions, including four to the king of France and one to the Holy Roman Emperor, Maximilian I. In the thirteenth year of his service, a French invasion toppled the Florentine government, and he was forced into exile. It was then that he wrote his book. By writing it, Machiavelli hoped to gain favor with the new rulers of Florence and win back his job. They ignored him. Nevertheless, *The Prince* became the most famous book on political science ever written, and it is still read by politicians today.

Machiavelli lived when ruthless kings and queens united territories with a shared language into larger centralized kingdoms. This was the first time in European history that this occurred. Prior to the fifteenth century, most of Europe was divided into countless small territories ruled by noblemen. In some instances, these territories were organized into kingdoms. However, the kings were often too weak to challenge the power of the nobility. As a result, people who lived in a region with the same language might find themselves governed by several different rulers. In the late Middle Ages and Renaissance, powerful monarchs emerged who could outsmart or defeat the nobility. The kingdoms created by these strong rulers are called **nation-states** because all the people of one nationality were finally joined together under one king. In his writings, Machiavelli included many useful and realistic lessons based on the success of these cunning rulers.

According to Machiavelli, one of the most effective monarchs was Ferdinand of Spain. He began his career as crown prince of Aragon, one of the four kingdoms that would later unite to become modern Spain. In 1469, he married Isabella, queen of Castile. In the Renaissance, diplomacy often revolved around marriage between monarchs because it was an easy way to expand territory and win trustworthy allies. By marrying Isabella, Ferdinand united Aragon with the larger and richer kingdom of Castile. He also found in Isabella a highly intelligent, energetic, and determined wife with the same desire to strengthen royal power as himself. Together they set about curbing the power of the nobility. Instead of appointing nobles to positions in their government, they hired university-trained lawyers and churchmen who owed allegiance only to them. They also set up the **Hermandad**, a rural police force, to tackle disorder and carry law into the countryside. To increase respect for the monarchy, Isabella added ceremony and formality to the royal court. The Spanish learned to hold their king and queen in awe because they viewed them as living symbols of Spain.

But Spain was not yet fully united. There was still the emirate of Granada in the south. In 711, Spain was invaded by Moslem warriors from North Africa. The **Moors**, as these invaders were called, brought great learning and sophistication to Spain. Much of what medieval Europe knew about medicine, music, and philosophy was learned from the Moors. In addition to the Moors, a large Jewish population lived in Spain. They played crucial roles in the Spanish economy and society as craftsmen, traders, financiers, doctors, and scholars. Nevertheless, this was an age of religious warfare because Christians viewed Moslems and Jews as their enemies and vice versa. By 1491, only Granada remained in Moslem control. Ferdinand and Isabella joined forces and together drove the Moors from Spain in 1492.

Even before the conquest of Granada, Ferdinand and Isabella realized that Christianity could be used to further bind the Spanish people together and strengthen royal power. To accomplish this, they set up a kind of religious police force called the **Inquisition**. It was the Inquisition's job to make sure that all Spaniards were Christian. The Jews and the defeated Moors were given a choice: convert, die, or leave. Not surprisingly, most left.

The loss of Moslem and Jewish skills, knowledge, and creativity hurt Spain in the long run. In the short term, however, Ferdinand and Isabella succeeded in concentrating power in their hands and advancing the unification of Spain beyond their marriage. To their contemporaries, the finance of Columbus's voyage in 1492 seemed to be the least of their accomplishments. Upon their deaths, their daughter, Juana, inherited a powerful and cohesive state. It was this state under Juana's son, Charles V, that sent Spanish soldiers called **Conquistadors** to explore and conquer the new world. Machiavelli would have nodded his head with approval.

Name _____ Date _____

Challenges

1. Who wrote *The Prince?* _____

2. In the view of *The Prince,* why should a ruler choose to be feared more than loved?

_____

_____

3. Why should the Prince lie and cheat? _____

_____

_____

4. What was Machiavelli's job, and where was he sent? _____

_____

_____

5. What is a nation-state? _____

_____

6. What relationship was at the center of diplomacy in the Renaissance? _____

_____

7. Who did the Spanish rulers depend on for advisors in governing? Who did they leave out?

_____

_____

8. What professional contributions were made by the Jews in Spain? _____

_____

_____

9. What choice did the Inquisition give to non-Catholics? _____

_____

10. What was the short-term benefit of driving the Moslems and Jews from Spain?

_____

_____

Name _____ Date _____

Points to Ponder

1. Was Machiavelli evil? Explain.

_____

_____

_____

_____

_____

2. How are the lessons of Machiavelli's *The Prince* still practiced by modern politicians today?

_____

_____

_____

_____

_____

3. How do you think the expulsion of the Moors and Jews hurt Spain in the long run?

_____

_____

_____

_____

_____

Name _____ Date _____

Activities

1. Look at other examples of Machiavelli's writings on politics. He is surprisingly accessible. *The Horizon Book of the Renaissance* by J. H. Plumb has a good selection. Why is Machiavelli still read today?

2. Use the blank map of Spain on page 81 to complete the following activity.

   A. On the map provided, locate with a dot and label the following cities:
      1. Granada
      2. Madrid
      3. Barcelona
      4. Seville
      5. Toledo
      6. Valencia
      7. Salamanca
      8. Leon
      9. Cordoba

   B. On the map provided, locate and label these geographical formations:
      1. The Pyrenees Mountains
      2. Balearic Islands
      3. Atlantic Ocean
      4. Mediterranean Sea
      5. Bay of Biscay

   C. On the map provided, locate these nations:
      1. France
      2. Portugal

   D. On the map provided, locate these old kingdoms:
      1. Aragon (northeast Spain)
      2. Castile (central Spain)
      3. Granada (southeast Spain)
      4. Navarre (north-central Spain)

Name _____ Date _____

Map of Spain

Gloriana, Elizabeth's England

"Let tyrants fear! I have always so behaved myself that, under God, I have placed my chiefest strength and safeguard in the loyal hearts and good will of my subjects; and therefore I am come amongst you, as you see… resolved, in the midst and heat of the battle, to live or die amongst you all… ."

Thus spoke Queen Elizabeth I to her troops as they waited for a Spanish invasion of England. No doubt, her speech was followed by wild cheers because she was well-loved by her subjects. Elizabeth was one of the most successful of England's monarchs and had one of the longest reigns. The Elizabethan age, as historians call her reign, lasted from 1558 to 1603. It was an exciting time in which some of England's boldest adventurers and greatest poets and playwrights lived.

Elizabeth I

Dominating the age, however, was the queen. When Elizabeth came to power, England was suffering from a loss of self-confidence. England's confusion stemmed from thirty years prior to Elizabeth's reign when her father Henry VIII failed to produce a son. Henry's dynasty, the Tudors, were recent occupants of the throne and worried that other families with equally valid claims to the throne would unseat them. England did not yet have a tradition of ruling queens, and Henry feared that his only daughter, Mary, might lose the throne. Knowing that his wife of 17 years, Catherine of Aragon, was unable to have more children, Henry wanted his marriage annulled. He had already found a younger woman named Anne Boleyn to replace his wife, but he needed papal approval to dissolve the marriage. Unfortunately for Henry, the Pope at the time was controlled by Catherine's nephew, Charles V, King of Spain and ruler of half of Europe, as the Holy Roman Emperor. With such a powerful man influencing the Pope, Henry's request was denied.

Desperate, Henry took the dramatic step of breaking away from the Catholic church and forming his own called the Church of England. Europe was shocked. Henry then annulled his marriage to Catherine and married Anne. Henry's luck, however, had not changed. Anne bore him only another unwelcome daughter, Elizabeth. Ever more desperate, this time he executed his wife, Anne, so he could marry another woman, Jane Seymour. She gave birth to a sickly son named Edward. When Henry himself died in 1547, he had married three more times and left his kingdom divided and confused, especially over the nature of the Church of England.

Such a state of affairs was dangerous because religion was the central preoccupation of the age. It dominated politics and split the princes of Europe into two warring camps, Protestant and Catholic. Rulers were expected to choose the religious beliefs for their subjects, and those who disagreed with the king's choice were punished or exiled. Religious toleration was almost unknown in Europe. The **regents**, a governing board of men who ruled for ten-year-old King Edward VI, brought the Church of England into alignment with Protestant religious beliefs. Edward, however, lasted only five years before sixteenth-century medical care killed him. He was replaced by his older sister Mary, who was determined to make England Catholic again. Her efforts added to the nation's confusion. She, too, lasted only five years.

This was the realm that Elizabeth finally inherited. England's luck, however, had changed. At 25, Elizabeth was healthy and well-equipped to rule. She was courageous, intelligent, attractive, and charming. She had enjoyed a fine Renaissance education, which included mastery of Latin, Greek, French, and Italian. The previous reign gave Elizabeth her apprenticeship in the deadly game of Renaissance politics. Queen Mary I often suspected her younger sister of treason, and throughout Mary's reign, Elizabeth lived in fear of losing her head on the chopping block like her mother, Anne Boleyn. The experience taught Elizabeth prudence and insight into human character.

As we have seen, when Elizabeth came to the throne, she found an England that was dangerously divided by religious questions. One of her first accomplishments was the moderate Elizabethan religious settlement. This compromise made the Church of England Protestant but the ritual retained much of the ceremony and splendor of the Catholic church. Although the majority of Englishmen accepted the compromise, Elizabeth knew that some uncompromising Catholics and radical Protestants called Puritans would still reject the settlement. She tried to make life as easy for them as she could by demanding only that they conform outwardly to the new rules. As long as she could count on her subjects' loyalty, she did not desire "windows into men's souls."

With the religious settlement in place, Elizabeth inspired the loyalty of her people. She was a master of self-presentation and used the fact that she was a woman to her advantage. Her astonishing wardrobe was calculated to impress. Upon her death, she left over 2,000 magnificent dresses. With such devices, she encouraged her subjects to see her not only as a queen but as a goddess. Because she remained unwed, Elizabeth could also replace the Virgin Mary in the hearts of her subjects. With names like the Virgin Queen, Gloriana, or Diana, the goddess of the hunt, her subjects adored her.

With such a figure to inspire them, it is not surprising that some of the greatest writers in the English language lived during the Elizabethan age. The greatest of the age, however, was the playwright, William Shakespeare. His plays still appeal to modern viewers because of his deep understanding of human psychology. He is considered the greatest master of the English language that has ever lived. His enormous vocabulary, inventiveness, and poetry molded English literature and language.

Elizabeth was also served by men of action. Sir Walter Raleigh was the first to attempt to colonize North America. Sir Francis Drake raided England's enemy, Spain, wherever he could find Spanish shipping. The earl of Leicester lead an army into Holland to help the Dutch rebel against their Spanish overlords. It was the actions by men like Drake and Leicester that prompted an attempted Spanish invasion of England. A huge fleet called the **Spanish Armada** set sail in 1588 with the intention of conquering Elizabeth's England. But this was an England ruled by no ordinary queen. With the words of the speech that started this chapter still ringing in their ears, Elizabeth's navy drove the Armada into the wild North Atlantic where most of its ships perished.

Name _____ Date _____

Challenges

1. Who said: "Let tyrants fear"? _____

2. What were the two opposing forces in religion during the sixteenth century?

_____

_____

3. Which way did English rulers go in terms of religion during the reigns of Edward VI,

Mary I, and Elizabeth I? _____

_____

_____

4. What qualities did Elizabeth develop during Mary's reign? _____

_____

_____

5. What was the Elizabethan religious settlement? _____

_____

_____

6. What were radical Protestants called? _____

_____

7. How many dresses did Elizabeth own? _____

_____

8. What names were given to her by admiring subjects? _____

_____

_____

9. Who was the most famous playwright of Elizabeth's reign? _____

_____

10. What major naval battle did England win in 1588? _____

_____

Name _____ Date _____

Points to Ponder

1. Religion was important to politics in the sixteenth century. Should it be today?

_____

_____

_____

_____

2. How do you explain Elizabeth's success as a sixteenth-century queen?

_____

_____

_____

_____

3. What would Machiavelli have thought of Elizabeth?

_____

_____

_____

_____

Activities

1. Draw a cartoon satirizing Henry VIII's marital difficulties or the Tudor dynasty's flip-flops on religion.
2. Look at the portraits of Elizabeth found in *The Horizon Book of the Elizabethan World* by L. B. Smith. (Other biographies of the queen will do just as well.) What impression is she trying to create?
3. View episodes of the excellent BBC dramatization of Elizabeth's reign called *Elizabeth R.*

The Past and the Future

A good way to think about history is to imagine yourself standing in the middle of a huge oriental rug. Intricate designs of every possible shape are woven by threads of every possible color. Wherever you stand on the rug, the patterns and colors appear altered. Even the place where you once stood changes color as you look at it in a different light. Strolling along the rug, you also notice  that the patterns are ever-shifting. Nothing stays the same and yet nothing is ever completely new. One pattern's threads evolve into the next, sometimes quickly, sometimes slowly.

Just as the Renaissance contained colors and patterns from the preceding Middle Ages, so too the seventeenth century contained textures and shapes from the Renaissance. Historians call the seventeenth century the Baroque era to mark it off as a new age. Even so, it was laced with threads from the fifteenth and sixteenth centuries. Let's look at some of these threads as they revealed themselves in the years following the Renaissance.

The voyages of Christopher Columbus were but an early highlight in the history of exploration. Within 30 years of Columbus, Magellan rounded the southern tip of South America and crossed the Pacific Ocean. At approximately the same time, Hernando Cortes and a small Spanish army penetrated deep into Mexico to conquer the Aztec empire. Twenty years later in 1539, Hernando De Soto landed with another army on the coast of Florida and hiked as far north as North Carolina and crossed the Mississippi River in the west. These explorations brought Spanish Renaissance culture, in the form of government administrators, churches, and universities, to South and Central America.

Meanwhile, the same thirst for profit that caused fifteenth-century Florentines to establish banks, propelled seventeenth-century English investors to form trading companies. In 1607, the Virginia Company founded the first successful English colony in North America at Jamestown. Within a few years, this company established another colony that they hoped would be profitable. One hundred and one men, women, and children set sail in the *Mayflower* in 1620 in order to establish a colony at Plymouth. During their first winter, however, almost half the colonists died of disease and exposure. Why would people take such risks?

The answer lies in the fabric of the Reformation. The Pilgrims who settled at Plymouth were religious refugees fleeing persecution in a Europe divided by religion. At the end of the sixteenth century, the Protestants were split into many denominations that often squabbled with each other as much as they did with the Catholics. Furthermore, the Church of England was alarmed by Protestant extremists such as the Pilgrims and attempted to suppress their activities. Since the English king, James I, was the head of the Church of England, the Pilgrims had no choice but to flee. Life for Catholics in England had also been difficult for a long time. They too sought refuge in North America. In 1634, they founded St. Mary's, the first settlement in Maryland.

The scientific theories woven by Copernicus in 1543 had to wait another 60 years before they were finally confirmed by the Florentine scientist Galileo Galilei. In 1608, Galileo constructed a telescope in order to study the heavenly bodies. He identified the shadows of mountains on the Moon's surface, proved that the Sun turns on its own axis, and noted that Jupiter had moons that revolved around it like the planets revolve around the Sun. Within 50 years of this event, the governor of Connecticut, John Winthrop, Jr., was gazing at the same astonishing images in the first telescope brought to the North American colonies. Two generations later, Benjamin Franklin used the scientific method, so carefully crafted by Renaissance thinkers, to understand the nature of electricity.

In the broad tapestry of history, the Renaissance is still with us in countless ways. American cities are full of architecture modeled after Florentine churches and palaces of the fifteenth century. There are numerous performances of Shakespeare's *Romeo and Juliet* every year. Michelangelo's sculpture of David and Da Vinci's *Mona Lisa* continue to be held up as the height of human creativity. The threads from the fifteenth and sixteenth centuries run deep. Our language, our ideals, and our understanding of the world were shaped there. Whatever we see when we look at ourselves and the world around us has already been colored by the deep shades and rich hues of the Renaissance.

Activities

1. Look at pictures of Renaissance architectural styles. A good place to look is *The Panorama of the Renaissance* edited by M. Aston or *Gardner's Art Through the Ages* by R. G. Tansey or F. S. Kleiner. Then, go out into your community and see if you can find evidence of Renaissance-style architecture in local buildings.

2. Think about the history of your own life. What threads from the past run through it or even shape it? Can you locate threads that trace back to the Renaissance? Design and draw a diagram that shows the main influences that have come together to make you who you are.

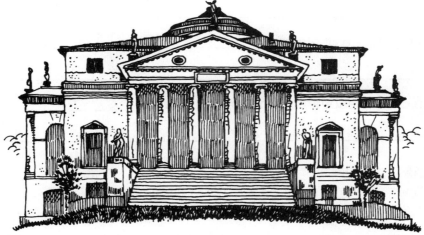

This villa was built in 1550. Can you see similarities between the Renaissance style and buildings constructed in the modern era? What elements in this structure were inspired by ancient Greek or Roman architecture?

87

Name _____ Date _____

Challenges

1. Who was the first to cross the Pacific? _____

_____

2. Who conquered the Aztec empire? _____

_____

3. What was the first successful English colony in North America? _____

_____

4. What ship brought colonists to Plymouth? _____

_____

5. Why were the Pilgrims anxious to leave England? _____

_____

_____

6. Who confirmed that Copernicus was right? _____

_____

7. How did the Renaissance affect American architecture? _____

_____

_____

8. What instrument astonished Governor John Winthrop, Jr.? _____

_____

9. Who studied the nature of electricity? _____

_____

10. What is one of Shakespeare's most popular plays? _____

_____

Name _____ Date _____

Points to Ponder

1. Why is it important to study history?

_____

_____

_____

_____

_____

_____

2. What threads from the Renaissance can you still see today?

_____

_____

_____

_____

_____

_____

3. What would an educated person from the Renaissance think about today's politics, music, entertainment, religious practices, architecture, and art?

_____

_____

_____

_____

_____

_____

Answer Keys

Good News for the City of Florence, The Late Middle Ages (page 3)

1. A ruthless duke of Milan who tried to conquer Italy
2. Italy was made up of tiny, independent city-states, while the rest of Europe had kings.
3. Peace and security
4. To give people protection in time of war
5. Peasants gave up their possessions and freedom to a local feudal lord who offered the protection of his castle in return.
6. Gunpowder made war more expensive.
7. Trade
8. Spices, medicines, and luxurious cloth
9. They were close to the Middle East, and they had well-developed urban environments.
10. Walled cities and democratic ideals

The Medici Rule, Patronage (page 9)

1. The city roused itself against the conspirators.
2. The ruling council of Florence
3. They were willing to murder, pillage, and exile their opponents.
4. The Medici banking business had 16 branches in European cities.
5. Giovanni spent money on churches and founding hospitals.
6. He was banker to the city and special advisor to the government.
7. They were bankers and charged interest, which was considered a sin in the fifteenth century.
8. They spent huge amounts of money on churches, palaces, costly furniture, and elegant clothing.
9. Giants on stilts and people dressed up like pagan gods, etc.
10. Lorenzo

In the Courtyard of the Medici Palace, The Early Renaissance (page 13)

1. Ancient statues of Roman emperors and Greek philosophers, tapestries of Greek mythology, beautifully bound books by ancient authors, etc. (any three)
2. Rebirth
3. It was a new appreciation for the art, architecture, and literature of ancient Greece and Rome.
4. Those who embraced Renaissance ideas
5. Classical writers believed that humans had great potential for growth in all areas. They were concerned with living this life fully. They believed in an active and creative life. They believed that the human body was beautiful.
6. He perfected his Latin, collected ancient manuscripts, and wrote letters comparing his own day to that of the ancient world. He also

wrote love poetry and served on diplomatic missions.
7. Homer, Virgil, and Cicero
8. The *Decameron*
9. Leonardo Bruni and Marsilio Ficino

The Bronze Head, The Early Renaissance (page 17)

1. The same as craftsmen or artisans
2. They wanted to create an image of sophistication, elegance, and piety.
3. In Florentine workshops that produced gold jewelry and silver work
4. The Gothic style
5. In the Gothic cathedral
6. Everything in the cathedral was to move the viewer's eye upward and away from the earth toward heaven.
7. He used symbols to tell a biblical story or convey a religious truth.
8. They wanted to follow in the footsteps of classical artists and create images of the world as it ordinarily looked. They also wanted to bring the classical spirit back to life.
9. Rome
10. Masaccio, the painter, and Brunelleschi, the architect, accompanied Donatello. They studied all that they could find in the ancient ruins of Rome.

The Dome, The Early Renaissance (page 21)

1. 1436
2. They had forgotten how.
3. Eight ribs hold up the dome from within.
4. It was a huge arm made of stone that came out from the wall and propped up medieval cathedrals.
5. Balance and harmony
6. They believed that the external environment had a profound impact on the mind and body of ordinary people.
7. Creating images of the world that look realistic
8. Linear perspective
9. He used rules of proportion and experimented with light and shadow.
10. The *David* was the first free-standing nude sculpture since classical times. It portrayed David as a beautiful adolescent standing triumphantly upon the huge helmeted head of Goliath.

Leonardo da Vinci, The Renaissance Man (page 25)

1. Verrocchio
2. Leonardo painted a more life-like angel than his teacher had been able to paint.
3. The *Mona Lisa* and the *Last Supper*
4. The 5,000 pages of Leonardo's notebooks

5. Central heating, machine guns, submarines, tanks, life preservers, airplanes, parachutes (any five)
6. He gained knowledge by looking closely at the physical world.
7. Sickness occurred when one of the four humors dominated the rest.
8. His attempt to try new ways to mix paint
9. At the court of the king of France
10. First, we can only command nature when we understand her. Second, we must learn about nature by observation. Third, the physical world cannot be understood by relying upon huge, all-encompassing theories, but rather by close observation of detail.

Michelangelo and the High Renaissance (page 29)

1. He surrendered the castles around Florence to the French.
2. The Florentines drove the Medici from the city and pillaged the Medici palace.
3. France and Spain
4. By siding with one side and then the other
5. He studied in the Medici household.
6. Sculpture
7. Life was like a block of uncarved marble, and the soul was trapped within it. Every human being, like a tireless artist, had to work at releasing the soul's perfection.
8. The *David*
9. 6,300 square feet
10. The stories from Genesis

Education and the Renaissance Woman (page 33)

1. Ferrara
2. In childbirth
3. It should be well-rounded and include education of the mind and the body.
4. History, literature, grammar, rhetoric, logic, music, dancing, riding, and fencing
5. Greek and Latin literature
6. Mainly upper-class males
7. They learned a smattering of classical literature, music, and dance. They also learned how to manage a household, do needlework, be religious, and be a good wife.
8. They were married off to other princes in order to create alliances, and they were supposed to give birth to children to keep the family alive.
9. They were married between the ages of 13 and 16 to much older men.
10. She used skillful diplomacy and strict control of the army.

The Life of the Lower Classes in the Renaissance (page 38)

1. In the countryside
2. All had to do hard work. They had bad teeth

90

and were often ill from malnutrition. Starvation was always a possibility.

3. They feared starvation on the road.

4. Church holidays, weddings, seasonal rituals, and occasional fairs

5. They were exposed to beautiful architecture, art, and ideas.

6. Rarely over 100,000 people

7. Because most were walled

8. Streets were unpaved, narrow, and crooked. They were also crowded with livestock, peddlers, and wagons.

9. They had no street lights.

10. It killed about one-third of the population of Europe.

The Northern Renaissance (page 42)

1. Donatello and Brunelleschi

2. Gothic painting; it looked mystical and dream-like. Spatial proportions often appeared unnatural in order to emphasize the symbolic importance of a figure.

3. Germany was divided up into dozens of semi-independent states. Also, the German states thrived on trade, and rich banking families were willing patrons of the arts. Germans were also fascinated with nature.

4. Venice

5. The techniques of drawing realistically and admiration for Greek and Roman literature

6. It had not yet split into Protestant and Catholic churches.

7. The widely-used Latin translation of the Bible.

8. They began to criticize the way the Bible was translated and interpreted.

9. A Dutch humanist who published a New Testament in Greek that differed in meaning with the Vulgate.

10. A different translation of the Bible

The Printing Press (page 48)

1. Death, Famine, War, and Plague

2. Woodblock printing

3. China

4. 100 calfskins or 300 sheepskins

5. Johann Gutenberg

6. Suddenly, many more people had access to much more information.

7. English, French, Spanish, and Italian

8. Religious books, ancient classics, grammar books, law books, astrology handbooks, encyclopedias, almanacs, and chivalric romances

9. It helped the vernacular languages to develop their own literature.

10. More people had access to the ideals of ancient Greece and Rome. Other Europeans besides Italians could learn to look closely at nature and lead lives dedicated to human growth. They could also perfect their reading of Greek and Latin.

The Reformation (page 52)

1. Luther wanted to debate the sale of indulgences.

2. Documents sold by the church that were supposed to lessen the punishment for sinners in the afterlife

3. All Europeans belonged to one Christian church (the Roman Catholic church).

4. They owned almost a quarter of all farmland. Priests were exempt from taxation. They had their own laws and law courts. The clergy were almost the only people who could read.

5. It was too preoccupied with money and politics and was dominated by Italians.

6. German princes wanted to seize church property.

7. He translated the New Testament into German.

8. They believed that if Luther could defy the church, they could defy their landlords.

9. They preferred the rituals and ceremonies or admired the way the old church cared for the poor and sick.

10. It insisted upon better education for the priests, less preoccupation with wealth, and the end of the sale of indulgences.

Music and the Harmony of the Spheres (page 56)

1. The world is made of music.

2. Baldisarre Castiglione

3. The bagpipe and the hurdy gurdy

4. Lutes, viols, flutes, and harps

5. In ancient Greece

6. Flanders

7. Lorenzo de' Medici

8. They insisted that the words of a song were as important as the melody.

9. An Italian poem set to music for two or more voices

10. The printing press

Food, Feasts, and Manners (page 61)

1. A mythical animal created by sewing the upper part of a baked chicken onto the lower part of a roasted pig

2. Epiphany, Candlemas, Whitsunday, etc. (any three)

3. 17

4. Salmon belly, roast porpoise and peas, baked herring with sugar, etc. (any three)

5. Slapstick comedies

6. A noise-making prop used to hit actors for a laugh

7. Harlequino, Pantalone, and Il Capitano

8. Pastries, breads, and pies

9. They washed their fingers in bowls of lemon-scented water.

10. Cleaning teeth with a napkin, spitting, etc. (any two)

Fashion and Hygiene (page 66)

1. Because they plucked their hair

2. Only women from the lower classes had suntans.

3. Mercury, pearls, silver, and egg shells

4. Doublet or jerkin

5. With points

6. They believed it spread disease and that open pores allowed the body's vital forces to escape.

7. It was a way for the upper classes to mark themselves off from the lower classes.

8. Powder left on the head overnight and then combed out

9. Linen or hemp

10. It kept people clean.

A New Way of Looking at the Universe (page 70)

1. The earth

2. They were moved by angels.

3. They solved practical problems.

4. An alchemist

5. An astrologer

6. The natural philosophers

7. The Sun

8. Blood, phlegm, red and black bile

9. Medicine could cure illnesses, not bloodletting.

10. The Scientific Revolution

The Age of Exploration (page 74)

1. The caravel, the magnetic compass, and the astrolabe

2. Bartholomeu Dias

3. Ptolemy

4. China, Persia, Sumatra, and India

5. Venice

6. A new route to China

7. Cottons, silks, taffeta, muslin, damask, dye-stuffs, medicines, spices, perfumes, and pearls

8. Muslim warriors

9. Crusades

10. Prester John

Power: The Rise of the Nation-State and Machiavelli (page 78)

1. Machiavelli

2. It is safer to be feared.

3. For the good of the country

4. Ambassador sent to France and the Holy Roman Emperor

5. A nation where most of the people of one language are united under one government

6. Marriage

7. Lawyers and churchmen; they left out nobles.

8. They were traders, financiers, doctors, and scholars.

9. Convert, die, or leave

10. Spain was unified under a strong monarchy.

Gloriana, Elizabeth's England (page 84)
1. Elizabeth I
2. Catholics and Protestants
3. Edward VI—Protestant; Mary I—Catholic; Elizabeth I—Protestant
4. Prudence and insight into human character
5. The Church of England became Protestant, but the ritual retained the ceremony and splendor of the Catholic church.
6. Puritans
7. 2,000
8. Virgin Queen, Gloriana, or Diana
9. William Shakespeare
10. The defeat of the Spanish Armada

The Past and the Future (page 88)
1. Magellan
2. Hernando Cortes
3. Jamestown
4. The *Mayflower*
5. King James I was making their lives unbearable.
6. Galileo
7. Many buildings are modeled after Florentine churches and palaces.
8. The telescope
9. Benjamin Franklin
10. *Romeo and Juliet*

Bibliography

Aston, M. *Panorama of the Renaissance.* Singapore, 1996.
Burke, P. *Popular Culture in Early Modern Europe.* New York, 1978.
Bainton, R. H. *Here I Stand, A Life of Martin Luther.* Nashville, 1953.
Castiglione, B. *The Book of the Courtier.* London, 1967.
Fleming, W. *Arts and Ideas.* Chicago, 1991.
Fraser, A. *The Wives of Henry VIII.* New York, 1992.
Guy, J. *Tudor England.* Oxford, 1988.
Cosman, M. P. *Fabulous Feasts.* New York, 1992.
Duby, G. and Perrot, M. ed. *A History of Women in the West,* Vol. III. London, 1993.
Grafton, A. *New Worlds, Ancient Texts.* Cambridge, Massachusetts, 1992.
Hale, J. R. *Renaissance.* New York, 1965.
Hale, J. R. *The Civilization of Europe in the Renaissance.* New York, 1994.
Harris, N. *The Art of the Renaissance.* Bristol, 1995.
Hill, M. and Bucknell, P. *The Evolution of Fashion.* London, 1987.
Jacobs, A. *A Short History of Western Music.* London, 1973.
Jardine, L. *Worldly Goods, A New History of the Renaissance.* New York, 1996.
Jensen, D. *Renaissance Europe.* Lexington, 1992.
Jestaz, B. *Art of the Renaissance.* New York, 1995.
Machiavelli, N. *The Prince.* Oxford, 1952.
Morison, S. E. *Christopher Columbus, Mariner.* New York, 1954.
Murray, P. and L. *The Art of the Renaissance.* New York, 1963.
Nunn, J. *Fashion in Costume, 1200–1980.* New York, 1984.
Plumb, J. H. *The Horizon Book of the Renaissance.* New York, 1961.
Rabb, T. K. *Renaissance Lives.* New York, 1993.
Singman, J. L. *Daily Life in Elizabethan England.* London, 1995.
Smith, L. B. *The Horizon Book of the Elizabethan World.* New York, 1967.
Tansey, R. G. and Kleiner, F. S. *Gardner's Art Through the Ages.* New York, 1996.
Zophy, J. W. *A Short History of Renaissance and Reformation Europe.* Upper Saddle River, New Jersey, 1996.